# NOTHING
# SO KINGLY

## Darletta Martin

### CREEKSIDE CHARACTERS SERIES
Book One

# Nothing So Kingly

ISBN-10:   1-7361524-9-2
ISBN-13:   978-1-7361524-9-2

**USD Price**
$9.99
**In Canada**:
$12.95

**Order from: BOOK DEPOT**
Delmer & Darletta Martin
11508 White Hall Rd.
Smithsburg, MD 21783
Call: 301-791-6260
or 814-977-1280

**Cover Paintings:**
Phoebe Anthus

**Design:**
Illustra Graphics, Bedford, PA

Printed in the United States of America

# *Dedication:*

To my Flintstone schoolmates
with whom I shared the fancies of youth

If you see any likeness of yourself in this book,
consider it my recognition of your nobility.

**Acknowledgments:**

Many thanks to all my writer friends and their family members who freely shared advice and opinions on the first draft of this book. You know who you are!

Special honors to Lucrecia Mejia and Emily Steiner for doing thorough edits on the final version.

All characters in this story are fictional though some events are based on my childhood memories.

# TABLE OF CONTENTS

# NOBILITY

True worth is in being, not seeming,
In doing, each day that goes by,
Some little good—not in dreaming
Of great things to do by and by.
For whatever men say in their blindness,
And spite of the fancies of youth,
There's nothing so kingly as kindness,
And nothing so royal as truth.

We get back our mete as we measure—
We cannot do wrong and feel right,
Nor can we give pain and gain pleasure,
For justice avenges each slight.
The air for the wing of the sparrow,
The bush for the robin and wren,
But always the pathway is narrow
And straight, for the children of men.

'Tis not in the pages of story
The heart of its ills to beguile,
Though he who makes courtship to glory
Gives all that he hath for her smile.
For when from her heights he has won her,
Alas! It is only to prove
That nothing's so sacred as honor,
And nothing so loyal as love!

We cannot make bargains for blisses,
Nor catch them like fishes in nets;
And sometimes the thing our life misses
Helps more than the thing which it gets.
For good lieth not in pursuing,
Nor gaining of great nor of small,
But just in the doing, and doing
As we would be done by, is all.

Through envy, through malice, through hating,
Against the world, early and late,
No jot of our courage abating—
Our part is to work and to wait.
And slight is the sting of his trouble
Whose winnings are less than his worth;
For he who is honest is noble,
Whatever his fortunes or birth.

*—Alice Cary*

# CREEKSIDE FAMILIES

Donovan & Cynthia Wadel

| **Darica** | 14 | **Grade 9** |
|---|---|---|
| **Danielle** | 12 | **Grade 7** |
| Landon | 9 | Grade 4 |
| Lashonda | 6 | Grade 1 |
| Brenton | 3 | |
| Britney | 1 | |

Elwood & Rosalie Kurtz

| Stephanie | 21 | |
|---|---|---|
| Veronica | 18 | |
| **Trevor** | 15 | **Grade 10** |
| **Emelisa** | 13 | **Grade 8** |
| Brady | 6 | Kindergarten |

James & Judy Ebersole

| Jayden | 18 | |
|---|---|---|
| **Jolene** | 12 | **Grade 7** |
| Jarrett | 6 | Grade 1 |

Larry & Mabel Amstutz

| Gary | 18 | |
|---|---|---|
| Roger | 16 | |

*Larry & Mabel Amstutz (Continued)*

| | | |
|---|---|---|
| **Waylan** | 13 | **Grade 8** |
| **Everett** | 11 | **Grade 6** |
| Quentin | 9 | Grade 4 |
| Megan | 6 | Grade 1 |
| Othniel | 3 | |
| Cordell | 1 | |

Willis & Cheryl Brubaker

| | | |
|---|---|---|
| Cheyenne | 7 | Grade 2 |
| Winston | 4 | |
| Chantelle | 1 | |

Roland & Shana Meyers

| | | |
|---|---|---|
| Carlin | 8 | Grade 3 |

Mose & Fern Meyers
(former teacher, Roland's father)

| | |
|---|---|
| Mark | 24 |

Ernest & Alma Wadel
(minister, Donovan's father)

# NOTHING SO KINGLY

## Darletta Martin

CREEKSIDE CHARACTERS SERIES
Book One

# NOTHING SO KINGLY

CHAPTER ONE

## Story-telling Sister

Darica took two diapers from her little sister Lashonda, who immediately reached into the gray Rubbermaid laundry tub for another handful. Clipping the clothes pins in place, she continued the story she was telling in return for Lashonda's help.

"And Katie had a clothesline just like this, except hers was on the roof of the canal boat instead of in the backyard, and she had to climb up a little ladder to hang up her baby sister's diapers. She hung up the bed sheets, too—" Darica gestured toward the sheets swaying in the faint August breeze. "But their sheets weren't as big as ours, because they used straw ticks for their mattresses—one for the girls, another for the boys, and a bigger one for their parents who slept in a little curtained-off room in the stern.  That's the back end of the boat, you know."

Lashonda handed Darica more diapers.  "Where did their baby sleep?"

"In a clothes basket beside her parents' bed."

"A basket like this?" Lashonda pushed the tub with her foot.

"No, they didn't have plastic stuff like this.  They had a wicker basket like the one Grandma keeps dolls in."

Lashonda nodded.  "But then Katie could only hang up wash when Bea wasn't sleeping, or else they had to lay Bea on somebody else's bed."

"Good thinking!" Darica grinned at Lashonda. This sibling wouldn't be a dense first grader.

Lashonda had another question. "Did they have a washing machine on the boat?"

"No.  All they had was a big wooden tub and a scrub board.  You know, like in the Laura and Mary books."

"Oh, yeah!" Lashonda's eyes sparkled.  "I remember when you read me them stories."

"Those stories," Darica corrected automatically. "Anyway, Katie got so tired of—"

"Hey, Lashonda!" Landon skidded his bike to a stop beside them.  "Can you come ride bike with me? I'm playing that I'm chopping corn, and I need you to run a silage cart."

Lashonda thrust the diaper she was holding into Darica's hand. "You can tell me some more later," she called over her shoulder as she ran for her bike.

Darica grinned. At least she had gotten five minutes' worth of help from Lashonda. Ever since the school's field trip to the C&O Canal, she had been creating one story after another about Katie who lived on a canal boat. Her siblings begged for these stories every time they worked together. When she worked alone, Darica usually spent her time imagining.

By now, Katie and her family seemed like friends who lived in the neighboring county. Darica wished she could write Katie a letter and ask for an update on her life. She would also ask her more details about being Irish. Because that's what Katie's family was, of course. The eighth-grade history book said Scotch-Irish immigrants often took jobs on the railroads and canals, and Darica had read a series of books about a delightful Irish family. That was how she knew what names to use for Irish people.

She was particularly fond of the character she had invented as Katie's brother Sean. She would make up another adventure of his right now to tell

Landon while they fed calves this evening. *Sean*. Darica liked the looks of that spelling better than *Shawn*. It made the boy tall and lean rather than short and fat.

When she had started reading the Irish family series, she had pronounced the name *Seen*. Then Emelisa had unknowingly enlightened her by pronouncing *Sean* just like *Shawn* when reading a sentence from their English book at school. So, *Sean* was the Irish spelling. What a relief that she hadn't been the one reading aloud!

The back door banged, and Danielle came across the yard with more laundry. "Only four weeks until school starts," she said, plopping her tub on the grass. She picked out the first pair of pants and flapped them straight. "When do you think we'll ever find out who's teaching?"

"Today, I hope," Darica answered. "Can you imagine anybody besides Brother Mose behind the teacher's desk?"

"Hardly, but it would be fun to have somebody young enough that he doesn't complain about back pain every day."

"Or blame his forgetfulness on brain shrinkage!" Danielle laughed.

"What if Daddy has to teach?" Darica made a face.

"He said one of the school board members will have to if they can't find anybody else."

Danielle kept adding to the row of pants. "He's too busy farming."

Darica pinned the last diaper to the line, grabbed the tub by one handle, and strolled toward her sister, counting diapers aloud as she went. "Twenty-three!" she announced. "We must have exactly two dozen, because Mom said Britney is wearing the last clean one. Hope they dry fast, or Mom will have to use a disposable, and you know how wasteful she thinks that is. Diapers make such a neat, symmetrical row. Don't you feel sorry for anybody who never gets to hang them out?"

Danielle nodded. "Like Jolene?"

"Yeah." Darica snorted. "And her opinionated mother. Remember all that stuff she said about diapers being so unsanitary?"

"Jolene said her mom would buy Pampers if she had to do it with her last cent," Danielle remembered.

"Poof! What sense does that make, as rich as they are? And why are they still talking about diapers when Jarrett is ready to start first grade?"

"Beats me. Maybe they just now got him trained," Danielle joked. "Do you think he'll do any better in school than Jolene does? I mean, I like her for a friend, but she just isn't much good at lessons."

"Money can't buy brains," Darica said. "But she'll have four new dresses to start the school year, and we won't get more than one before we're through the canning season. I'm glad I have two nice ones left from last year. Is your basket empty?"

Danielle held up the last pair of pants. "At least we aren't out here making up stories this time," she giggled. "Mom said she'd get our dresses finished sooner if we'd stop telling stories and work faster."

Darica hurried toward the house. "I can work fast and make up stories at the same time. Anyway, we're finished the laundry now, so let's ask Mom if we can fix lunch while she sews."

# NOTHING SO KINGLY

CHAPTER TWO

## Mini Barn Builder

"Wish Dad didn't like to talk so much," Trevor muttered to the mini barn door as he marked the spots for hinges. He glanced at his watch and frowned toward the closed office door through which Dad and the customer had disappeared twenty-eight minutes ago. At the supper table, they would hear all the subjects Dad had covered besides a mini barn order.

All the while, Trevor was stuck with the work—alone. Building barns wasn't so hard, but it got boring. Too bad he didn't have a brother. Well, he did have Brady, but how much did he count when it came to help? He could dismantle faster than Trevor could build.

Scowling, Trevor began to assemble the door latch. After twelve years of life with three sisters, he had been excited about adopting Brady from Romania. But how could he have known that Dad and Mom would not be able to train Brady like a normal child? No one had warned them that Brady's brain had been damaged by his birth mom's use of alcohol and his chaotic life in an orphanage. Three years later, spankings still sent him into fits of rage and taught him nothing. Time-out lasted less than two minutes. Limiting Brady's food or fun was ineffective, because he didn't care about them anyway.

At first, Trevor had welcomed his new brother to share his bedroom, but finally he had run out of tolerance for ruined property and stinky carpet. When Dad agreed to finish out the upstairs closed-in porch to make a new room, Trevor had nearly worn out his legs carrying tools, boards, and paneling up the stairs. Brady still messed with his stuff sometimes. The worst was that when Trevor tried to stop him from drowning a cat or dumping BB's in the sandbox, Brady promptly socked him in the stomach.

As usual, thinking about Brady brought him on the scene. Tearing through the open garage door at the end of the shop, he yelled, "Dad! Dad!"

Trevor stepped into his path and put out both hands. "Whoa. Is the house on fire?"

"No. I want Dad."

"He's talking to a customer."

"I don't care." Brady shoved past Trevor and slammed against the office door. "Dad! Dad!" He beat on the door with both fists.

Dad opened the door. "What, Brady?"

"Come right now."

"Let me finish this first." Dad attempted to shut the door, but Brady plowed headfirst through the narrow opening. Trevor knew he'd be really sweet inside, trying to impress the customer with his cuteness.

Trevor sighed and rolled his eyes as he picked up the cordless drill. Sometimes he wished he didn't have to go back to school for tenth grade, but at least he would get a break from Brady. Too bad Mom and the lower grade teacher were planning for Brady to do some kindergarten this year. Trevor hoped Brady would put his best foot forward at school—without kicking.

# NOTHING SO KINGLY

## CHAPTER THREE

## Dog Scrubber

"Sit, Nickie!" Jolene commanded, stuffing the ten-week-old puppy into the weighing basket. "I have to know how much you grew this week."

The Siberian husky stretched up to lick Jolene's hand.

"I taste like dog food, huh?" She wrote Nickie's weight on the memo board beside the scales; Father would want to include it in the next ad. "Done with you now." She put the black and white pup back inside the kennel and selected another of Annie's babies.

"Balto, you need a bath before the Kramers see you. You'll probably get hauled off to a new home today." She cuddled Balto in one arm and stroked the white hair between his pointy ears. The water in the wash tub—doggy spa, as Jayden called it— should be the right temperature by now. She had run more hot water in than she intended.

As she lowered the squirming dog into the water, a sudden memory flashed through her mind of Danielle sitting in the desk across the aisle from hers, telling how much fun she had bathing and dressing her baby sister. As she struggled to keep Balto in his bathtub and scrub him at the same time, she pictured Britney with her round cheeks and curly hair. How privileged Darica and Danielle were to have two charming little sisters—and two brothers besides! They told so many stories about the fun they had. Jolene had thought it ridiculous when Danielle complained about needing to babysit when she wanted to read a book. Books were boring compared to babies! Even if she had to hang out diapers like Danielle did, she would be glad for a baby sister.

That thought triggered another memory—one that made Jolene's face turn hot. Why had she ever repeated her mother's words about cloth diapers being gross? Danielle and Darica probably thought that was a dumb thing for her to say when her family had no baby. But how could they understand Mother's hatred for dirt? Mother cleaned and tidied the house all the time, but it never satisfied her. She kept talking about the big, new house they would build when they had saved enough money from Father's business.

"Yow!" Jolene yelped as Balto flailed in the tub. Water splashed over the edge and soaked the front of her dress.  Look what she got for daydreaming while bathing a dog!  As she lifted the dripping puppy out and flipped a towel around him, a story line popped into her head, "The old woman under the bridge lived a dog's life—nothing to sleep on but rags, nothing to gnaw but bones."

"You live better than that, don't you, Balto?" She rubbed the puppy dry. "But that's how I feel some- times—like I live a dog's life. Mother wants every- thing so perfect, but I spend most of my time raising dogs while she manages the house. I wish she'd teach me to cook and sew and do my lessons better..."

Carrying Balto to a clean kennel, she penned him in to wait for his showing.  As she emptied the wash tub, she recalled who had written that sen- tence about a dog's life: Darica, who wrote the best stories of anyone in school.  Another reason to be jealous of Danielle—she had a such a smart sister.

A yell from the paved driveway interrupt- ed her envy. "Look at me, Jo!"

She looked up to see Jarrett wobbling toward her on the Ripstick he had gotten for his sixth birthday.

"Hey!" She clapped for him. "You're doing it!"

Jarrett clattered to a stop against the side of the kennel, his sweaty face shining. "I learned in three days!"

Jolene grinned. "You're super! I wish I could do that."

"Want to try it?" He pushed the Ripstick toward her.

Jolene glanced toward the house. Was Mother watching? Tentatively, she stepped onto the wheeled apparatus, bracing her hands against the kennel. The next instant, she landed in a heap. When she looked up at Jarrett, the surprise on his face set her giggling. "Don't worry! I'm not broken!"

Jarrett started laughing, too. "I didn't know you would fall down so soon! Here's how you do it." He hopped back on the Ripstick and waved his arms to balance himself.

"At least I have one funny little brother," Jolene whispered as he lurched away.

# NOTHING SO KINGLY

CHAPTER FOUR

## Baby Sitters

"Go back to sleep," Waylan whispered, patting his little brother. "You're okay." He found the rocking horse quilt bunched in the corner of the crib and tucked it around Cordell. The baby's whimpers stopped. By the glow of the nightlight, Waylan watched him turn his head and plug his left thumb into his mouth, his eyes closed.

Waylan flopped down on his bunk and waited until Cordell's breathing changed to the even rhythm of sleep. He had heard Dad and the older boys go to the barn a half hour ago, so Everett and he should soon go out to feed the calves and heifers. But Dad would agree that caring for Cordell came first, so Mom could rest longer.

Waylan lifted himself noiselessly from the mattress and reached up to wake Everett in the bunk above him. They found their clothes in the darkness and slipped out of the room without waking Quentin and Othniel in the other bunk bed. Not many families had five boys sleeping in one room, but at least it was bigger than the tiny one where Megan slept alone. Waylan often wondered what it would be like if he had several older sisters like Trevor did. A big sister would do the housework when Mom was sick. But he'd rather manage Othniel and Cordell any day than Trevor's brother Brady.

Downstairs, they checked the pantry. "Not a cookie in sight," Everett complained.

"You'll have to make some today." Waylan dug into a pretzel bag. He tried not to think of all the food Mom used to make before she felt sick so often.

Everett did a thumbs-up. "I hope I have time." He loved anything that had to do with food.

Boots on, they headed for the calf barn. Waylan grinned as he switched on the light and watched the calves come to life, bawling and frisking around their pens in anticipation of breakfast.

"Your turn to get milk." Everett picked up a grain bag.

Waylan grabbed two empty five-gallon buckets and went out the open door at the other end of the calf barn. A short cut through the barnyard was the quickest way to the milking parlor.

Dad greeted him with a cheerful good-morning when he entered, but Roger grumped, "About time you get here. We milked yesterday's fresh cow, and there's another one to round up."

Waylan lifted the stainless-steel pail used for milking antibiotic-treated cows and poured the contents into one of his buckets. He wondered if Roger was worried about Mom's upcoming doctor appointment. Aloud he asked, "How do you know there's another one?"

"Gary saw her when he brought the cows in," Dad explained. "It's 874. She's still in the dry cow pasture, and you'll have to catch the calf, too."

"No problem." Waylan liked that kind of challenge.

"If you need help, holler for Gary. He's probably about done mixing the TMR."

In the milk house, Waylan dipped out a bottle of colostrum-rich milk for the fresh cow's calf and added milk from the line for the other calves.

Fifteen minutes later, as the sun burst over the mountain, he and Everett jumped into the pickup and drove out the field lane to the dry cow pasture.

"There she is!" Everett pointed at the cow lowing along the fence.

"The calf must be on this side the way she's acting," Waylan said.

"I don't see him anywhere."

"Why don't you jump out and chase the cow down to the gate? I'll drive to the top end of the pasture and loop back. That calf can't be very far away from its ma." Waylan paused with his foot on the brake while Everett hopped out.

Everett urged the cow downhill. Waylan drove slowly, scanning the hayfield on one side and the pasture on the other.

"Hey, look! There he is!" Everett hollered, pointing at the compost pile to the left of the lane.

It took Waylan a moment to catch on; then he laughed. Somehow the calf had climbed to the top of the lumpy mound of manure, soil, and moldy silage that covered the decaying carcasses of farm animals. There he lay, as comfortably bedded as if he had found a straw heap.

Everett darted out from under the electric fence. "I'll chase him down to you! Be ready!"

Waylan jumped out of the truck and stood at the bottom of the pile, expecting the calf to come down in the direction it was facing. But the calf whipped around and dashed down the other side.

Everett doubled over laughing. "He didn't like the looks of you!"

Waylan tore after the calf and grabbed him by the tail. It bawled and ran more wildly, but Waylan hung on. "Bring the truck!" he yelled to Everett.

The calf wore out at last, and with one brother working the head end and the other the tail end, they hoisted him onto the truck bed. "Now you sit on him while I drive in," Waylan puffed. "Then I'll help you with the cow."

"I'm a great baby sitter!" Everett straddled the prone calf.

Waylan laughed. It did seem that he and Everett had been appointed the farm and family baby sitters. Well, they mostly did a good job of it.

# NOTHING SO KINGLY

CHAPTER FIVE

## New Teacher

"Did I hear somebody drive in?" Darica asked as she drained the dishwater after lunch. Lashonda dropped her dish towel and ran to the window.

"Grandpap's are here!" Landon shouted in through the screen.

Within minutes, the whole family had gathered on the porch to meet Grandpap and Grandmother Wadel. Grandpap opened the sliding door on his minivan and lifted out his familiar plastic crate. The children knew what that meant. Darica and Danielle grinned at each other. Landon and Lashonda danced and shouted, "Books! More books!" Brenton and Britney nearly tumbled off the porch trying to reach their grandparents first.

Grandmother caught Britney and gave her a hug.

"We went to the sale at Booksavers this morning."

"And I found something for each of you." Grandpap set his crate on one of the wide concrete steps and sat down beside it. "Here's yours, Britney." He handed the toddler a chunky board book with baby animals on the cover. "And this is for you, Brenton." He held out a colorful copy of *We're Going on a Bear Hunt.*

Lashonda planted herself in front of Grandpap. "Soon I'll know how to read."

Grandpap smiled at her. "I remembered that, so I got you this." He picked up an Alice and Jerry primer. "This was my first reading book."

"You mean it's that old?" Lashonda's eyes widened as she reached for it.

"No, I meant it's like the books we had in first grade." Grandpap reached into his crate again and pulled out *The Bobbsey Twins.* "Have your read this, Landon? It was one of my childhood favorites. Sorry this copy's a bit tattered, but maybe your mom can cover it with plastic. They're hard to find anymore."

"That's okay." Landon took his book happily. "Thank you. I never read it before."

"And I couldn't decide which of these you big girls would want, so I guess I'll let you choose." Grandpap held out *The Winged Watchman and One Hundred and One Famous Poems.*

"We'll read each other's anyway," Danielle said, reaching for the storybook. "I know Darica has wanted that poem book for a long time." She looked at her sister. "Isn't that the one you were talking about?"

"Yes!" Darica took the slender volume and admired its mahogany hardcover. "This looks classic! Thanks so much, Grandpap! I always like hearing you read these poems."

Grandpap smiled. "I guess you inherited your love of poetry from me. My favorite in that book is 'Nobility' by Alice Cary. You'll find it on page iii."

Darica found the poem and held out the book. "Will you read it aloud right now, please?"

"Sure." Grandpap took the book. His booming voice rang across the lawn the same way it did when he was preaching.

> "True worth is in *being*, not *seeming*,
>   In doing, each day that goes by,
>   Some little good—not in dreaming
>   Of great things to do by and by.
>   For whatever men say in their blindness,
>   And spite of the fancies of youth,
>   There's nothing so kingly as kindness,
>   And nothing so royal as truth..."

Darica thrilled to the musical words. *I'm going to read that poem until I understand it, and then I'm going to memorize it*, she determined.

· · · · ·

"Well, girls, you finally have the promise of a teacher for this term." Daddy stood at the front of the milking parlor and grinned at Darica and Danielle as he slid his phone back into his pocket.

Darica had been telling the next chapter of "Katie's Canal Boat" to Danielle while they milked, but this topic was more important. "Who? Do we know him?"

"Willis Brubaker. He taught in Ghana for a few years. They just came back to Crystal Springs, and he was looking for a job."

"Are they going to move here?" Danielle asked.

"Probably. Fifty miles is pretty far to drive each day." Daddy opened the gate so Darica could chase the row of cows out.

Darica slapped the cows to hurry them along. "Is there a place they can rent?"

"Elwood suggested that little house on Ridge Road. It's close to school."

Darica raised her eyebrows. "That place is decrepit! Somebody would have to do some fast clean-up."

"Hey, that would be fun!" Danielle gave a bounce. "We and Elwood's girls and Jolene could all get together—"

"Huh! Jolene's mother wouldn't let her come within ten yards of that house," Darica interrupted. "You know Judy can't stand dirt and bugs and snakes."

"You're getting ahead of things," Daddy said. "Right now we need to finish the chores so I can get to board meeting by 7:00. Brother Willis agreed to come meet with us. He said he can't remember if he ever saw Creekside School, so he'd better find out what it looks like!" Daddy headed back to his barnyard scraping.

The girls shoved Katie's canal boat downstream while they discussed the new teacher.

"Brother Willis." Darica tried out the name as she took milkers off a row of cows. "He sounds tall and skinny, don't you think?"

"Not round like Brother Mose, anyway." Danielle grabbed the post dipper. "Do you know his wife's name?"

"Cheryl. I remember from the Ghana reports. And they have two little children named Wilhelmina and Charlemagne."

"Are you serious? That sounds like—like English royals, or whatever you call the kings and queens."

Darica burst out laughing. "I totally made that up! I just thought it would be clever, because they would start with *W* and *Ch* like their parents."

"You and your wild ideas for names! I hope you don't name your children anything that my children won't approve of."

Darica opened the exit gate. "Well, I'm glad I don't have a plain old name myself."

"Your name will be old by the time you're eighty." Danielle ran up the steps at the back of the parlor to chase more cows in. When she returned, she said, "I wonder if Brother Willis will think seven students are too many or not enough."

"Five grades will keep him busy." Darica pre-dipped the new row of cows. "I like having that many grades in a room instead of one or two like we had at Valley View. This way, we always have plenty of time to get our work done and read library books or write stories while the teacher is having class."

Danielle dried the cows Darica had dipped. "Except Jolene. She hardly ever gets her work finished."

"She's too particular. One time I watched her erase something about ten times." Darica started putting milkers on.

Danielle began at the other end of the row. "But her grades still aren't very good."

"That's why sometimes last year I asked Brother Mose if I could help her," Darica said. "I feel kind of sorry for her. I wonder what Brother Willis will think of everybody in our room."

The automatic take-offs were removing milkers from the other row of cows, so Danielle went to post dip them. "Everett will make him laugh. He says such comical stuff."

Darica mimicked, "Look, Dr. Miller, you can see the bone!" Everett liked to tell his classmates about the nurse's shock when she saw his cut chin. He still had a scar where the row of stitches had been.

"Brother Willis will also be impressed with how smart you and Emelisa are." Danielle opened the exit gate.

"You're just prejudiced." Darica grinned at her sister's flattery. "Waylan and Trevor are smart, too. They just didn't work very hard because Brother Mose didn't expect them to."

# NOTHING SO KINGLY

## CHAPTER SIX

## Dreading the Changes

Trevor shook his head as he stepped back from the office door. Shuffling to the half-built mini barn, he picked up a two-by-four. He hadn't meant to eavesdrop, but Dad had been talking on the phone, and Trevor couldn't help overhearing when he went to ask him a question: "So we finally have a teacher lined up. Willis Brubaker called just now and said he will do it... Yes, that's right... moved from Ghana to Crystal Springs... I suggested that house for rent on Ridge Road."

He guessed that Dad was talking to one of the other school board members, probably Donovan Wadel. He imagined Donovan hurrying to tell his family while putting his phone back into his pocket. From the way Darica and Danielle chattered at school, he got the impression that everybody in that family talked all the time and told each other everything.  He wondered how long it would be until Dad told him about the new teacher.  He would have to remember to act surprised.

Trevor grabbed the circular saw and buzzed the two-by-four to the right length.  Why did he feel so disgruntled?  Because he never had anybody to talk to?  He had gotten along with Brother Mose better than the other students had; Emelisa said it was because they were both pessimistic. What would Willis be like?  Young—if he was the Willis from Ghana—and busy with a family of little children. And now that Roger Amstutz was out of school, his only boy classmates would be Waylan in eighth grade and Everett in sixth.  If anybody could out-talk Darica and Danielle, those boys could.

Emelisa could never understand why he complained about their talkative classmates.  Though she was more reserved, she enjoyed their chatter. She was a good listener, Trevor thought, probably the easiest person for him to express himself to.

As if on cue, Emelisa called from the doorway of the shop, "Trevor!"

"Over here."  He stepped around the barn frame so she could see him.

"Did you hear who the new teacher is?  Dad just

came in and told Mom."

"Oh?" Trevor guessed Dad must have gone out the back door of the office to get to the house. Of course, he wouldn't come through the shop and tell his son first.

"It's Willis Brubaker who moved home from Ghana," Emelisa went on, never guessing that Trevor already knew. "Mom said his wife Cheryl is related to us somehow. They have three children. The oldest girl will be in second grade."

"Good thing they don't have another first grader," Trevor said dryly. "There are already three beginners, plus Brady."

Emelisa nodded. "But this makes an extra grade. Sister Suzanne wouldn't have had any second graders otherwise."

"Well, you and Darica can help her when you run out of work."

Emelisa grinned. "That would be fun. Do you think Brother Willis will be as easy on us as Brother Mose was?"

Trevor shrugged. "Probably not. And he won't have a clue what's wrong with Brady."

"Dad will explain to him," Emelisa said hopefully.

Trevor's stomach twisted. Not a good scenario.

Emelisa seemed to read his thoughts. "Don't

worry. Brady usually acts nice around strangers, you know."

Trevor snorted. "How long will the people at school be strangers? For the first two days, maybe."

"Emelisa!" Veronica called from the porch. "If you help me, we can pick the beans before supper."

"Okay," Emelisa replied. To Trevor she said, "Let's try not to worry about the school year yet. It probably won't be too bad."

Trevor watched her run to the garden and muttered, "She's obviously made of something different than I am."

# NOTHING SO KINGLY

CHAPTER SEVEN

## No A+'s

"What an adorable dog! I love this plume of a tail!" Mrs. Kramer gushed, cuddling Balto. "He's so fluffy and clean! How do you manage to raise such awesome dogs?"

Embarrassed, Jolene stammered, "Oh, it's just something I get lots of practice with. I mean, I take care of the dogs most of the time, and I like to have them looking nice for customers."

"Well, you sure deserve an A+ for this one!" Mrs. Kramer turned to Mother. "You can thank your daughter for getting me sold on this dog! Are you still asking the same price you listed in the ad?"

Soon the deal was complete. Mrs. Kramer laughingly held Balto up to give Jolene a good-bye kiss before she drove away.

Jolene was still smiling when Father appeared

at the kennel shed door. "You made a sale?" He looked at Mother.

"Yes. Mrs. Kramer. She made a fuss over Balto then tried to get a lower price. But I stuck with the one we listed in the ad."

Father nodded. "Good. We can't settle for less when we put as much into the dogs as we do. We'd soon be poor."

*Poor?* Jolene frowned as she poured fresh water into each dog's dish. Why did her parents always talk like that? *Poor* described her ability to do school work but not much else in her life.

"Do you have supper ready? It's six o'clock." Father liked a rigid schedule because of his welding and fabricating business. The sign on his shop door told customers he was not available between 6:00 and 6:30. Jolene didn't pay much attention to Father's work; she only knew that because he rarely turned down an opportunity to make money, he was always busy.

"Yes. Come on in. You, too, Jolene." Mother hurried to the house.

As Jolene turned her bucket upside down to dry, Father surprised her by saying, "I thought you might like to hear what Donovan told me when he stopped in for his new skid loader forks. He said they finally have a teacher hired."

"Who?"

"Willis Brubaker."

"I don't know him." Jolene picked at a mosquito bite on her arm as she followed Father to the house.

"I don't know much about him either, except that he and his family worked in Ghana for a while. I guess they were running out of money and came home to make some." He opened the door to the laundry room.

Mother set a fruit pizza on the table and came to the doorway. "Who are you talking about?"

"Willis Brubaker is coming to teach."

"They probably can't afford a house. Where will they live?"

"The school board is talking about renting the Ridge Road property for them."

Mother gasped. "Are you serious? I guess they got used to filth and poverty in Africa, but still..."

"I expect Elwood's and Donovan's families will put all kinds of time and money into cleaning it up. That's how they do things. Donovan thinks it's a sin to tear anything down."

Jolene half listened to the conversation as she took her place at the table. She watched Jarrett park his new *Fendt* tractor beside his toy barn and wondered if he would like school work any better than she did. Brother Mose had expected his students to manage without much help from him, so even with his lenient grading, she had gotten mostly B's and C's on her report card—never a line of A's like Mother had praised Jayden for earning. And of course, she never, ever made an A+ on a test like Danielle did when Darica helped her study. What would this new teacher think of her? Would he give her even worse grades?

During supper, her parents and brothers ate large servings of ham, mashed potatoes, and corn chip salad without noticing that Jolene ate only a few bites of each. How could anything taste good when a scary new school year loomed ahead?

Father and Jayden hurried out to the shop as soon as supper was over. Jarrett ran off to play. Mechanically Jolene cleared the table and started washing dishes. Mother always cooked and served the food. After the meal she put away the leftovers while Jolene did the dishes. They usually followed their routine without talking—another reason Jolene was jealous of Darica and Danielle.

This time, however, Mother had something on her mind. "Jolene, I didn't like your response to Mrs. Kramer's flattery. It sounded like bragging.

You don't need to act like the dogs are your project when Father and I put the money into them. We have taught you to feed and bathe them so that you have some chores to do. But people of the world don't understand our work ethics and might think we are giving you too much responsibility. The next time somebody starts talking so much, just keep quiet and let me decide what to say."

Jolene scrubbed dishes furiously, keeping her head bent to hide her tears. Working with dogs was the only place anybody had ever given her an A+. Now Mother was saying she didn't deserve even that. She had tried to reply politely, but Mother considered it bragging. As if Jolene had anything to brag about. Her stomach churned the few bites of supper she had swallowed. Mother obviously didn't think she was good for anything. Maybe Mother would rather not have a daughter.

# NOTHING SO KINGLY

CHAPTER EIGHT

## Heart Monitor

"I'll put the little boys to bed for naps if you let me have some of your cookies before we go to the barn," Waylan bargained.

"Sure." Everett dropped another ball of dough onto the cookie sheet. "I should have a nice pile baked by then." He opened the oven door and moved the first sheet from the bottom rack to the top before sliding another pan inside. "Mom mixed three kinds this morning, so I'll be busy for a while."

"She must not have felt too bad then."

"No, she said she felt okay this morning, but she thought she should still go to her doctor appointment." Everett frowned. "I hope there isn't anything wrong with her."

"But there must be some reason why she feels so weak and almost faints sometimes." Waylan scooped up Cordell who had been whining around his legs and took a sippy cup of milk from the refrigerator. "Come, Othniel. Naptime. I'll read you a story." The three-year-old trotted to the bookshelf for his favorite Richard Scarry book.

As they left the kitchen, Waylan heard the porch door slam and Megan ask, "Can I help you, Everett?"

Upstairs, Waylan tucked Othniel into his bunk and plopped down on the carpet, leaning his back against the bed. Cordell nestled against his shoulder, drinking his milk, while Waylan held the book up where Othniel could see the pictures.

By the time he finished the book, the little boys' eyes were drooping. Waylan gently laid Cordell in his crib and covered him. No matter how warm the summer day, the baby needed his favorite quilt for security.

Sighing with relief that they had cooperated so well, Waylan relaxed on his own bunk. He would just rest a little until they were sound asleep; then he would go down and help Everett.

When the sound of a vehicle in the driveway below woke him, he stared at the alarm clock in bewilderment. Three o'clock already! Dad and Mom must be home. He tiptoed across the room and down the stairs. He wanted to hear what the doctor had said about Mom, and yet he dreaded it. What if she had cancer or needed surgery?

Everett and Megan had dashed outside, leaving the oven door wide open.  Seeing at a glance that it was turned off, Waylan hurried out, too. Gary, Roger, and Quentin appeared from different directions as Dad and Mom got out of the van.  The children all stared at the device Mom was wearing on a strap over her shoulder.  It was hooked to several wires that disappeared inside her dress.  Dad motioned for Mom to sit down on the porch swing and sat down beside her.

"Are the little boys sleeping?" Mom asked.

Waylan felt relieved that her voice still sounded normal.  He nodded.  "I just came downstairs."

"Mom, what is that thing, huh?" Megan stood in front of the swing.

"It's a Holter monitor," Dad explained.  "Mom is supposed to wear it for twenty-four hours.  Then the doctor will read the record of how her heart beat during that time.  She is supposed to write down what she does—like eating, sleeping, and working.  That will help them figure out what is making her feel lightheaded and weak.  The doctor thinks she probably has an arrhythmia. That means her heart speeds up or slows down instead of beating with a regular rhythm."

"Will you need an operation?" Quentin asked.

"Hopefully not." Mom smiled. "But I might have to take medicine."

"I hope you get better before school starts," Everett said.

Waylan could hardly believe how they were all thinking the same thoughts. He had just been wondering if they should leave Mom alone without any help. Who would take care of the little boys when she couldn't?

"Talking about school," Dad looked at Waylan and Everett, "I wonder when they're going to find you boys a teacher."

"I guess if they don't, we'll just stay home and read books and help Mom," Waylan said. "We can learn just as much that way as we could at school."

# NOTHING SO KINGLY

## CHAPTER NINE

## Ridge Road House

"Well, girls, are you still excited about cleaning up the Ridge Road house?" Daddy
asked, coming into the kitchen where Darica
and Danielle were shaping butter rolls for school
lunches. Mom was mixing potato salad dressing
while overseeing Lashonda's egg-shelling.

"Sure! How bad is it? What will we do?" They
knew Daddy had gone with the rest of the
school board to assess the house.

"Bad enough. The owner said if we replace the
doors and windows that don't seal well, he'll lower
the rent. The renters had pets, so the carpets are
filthy, and there's dog and cat hair everywhere. The
worst part is the lean-to kitchen at the back. Its
roof leaked so long that the ceiling tile and insulation started falling down. The cupboards are

rotten, and there's trash everywhere, including moldy food. It stinks!"

The girls wrinkled their noses. Mom asked, "Why didn't somebody do something about it sooner?"

"Too much bother or not enough money, I guess. Anyway, we agreed to start this afternoon since we don't have much time before school starts."

Darica slid a pan of rolls into the oven and set the timer. "You need us right away?"

Daddy looked at Mom. "I'll be glad for their help, unless you need them."

"They may go with you. I'll sew while the little ones take naps."

"Elwood said his children can help haul out trash, too. He already called for a dumpster. So if you don't mind getting dirty and smelling bad smells..." Daddy looked at the girls.

Danielle giggled and quoted from a storybook, "'We'll have to wear clothes pins on our noses.'"

After lunch, Daddy, Darica, Danielle, and Landon loaded tools on the pickup and drove to Ridge Road. Elwood, Emelisa, and Brady were already there, propping doors and windows open.

"This place needs fresh air, or we'll suffocate!" Elwood called from the front door. "Trevor is bringing our skid loader, so we can throw the trash on the bucket and dump the stuff into the dumpster when it gets here."

Emelisa motioned for the girls to follow her inside. They gingerly crossed the threshold into the narrow foyer which opened into the living room. A rank odor assailed them.

"1 forgot my clothes pin!" Danielle sputtered, pinching her nose.

Darica spotted a ratty contraption of wood and carpet in one corner. "What's that?" she asked.

"Dad says it was for the cats. See all the claw marks here? And they could sleep on these padded carpet parts."

"There's the litter box underneath. Yuck, let's get that filthy stuff out of here."

"You can!"

"No, you!"

Darica and Emelisa stood laughing and raising their eyebrows at each other.

Danielle came up with a solution. "Hey, Landon, you're strong enough to move this, aren't you?"

"Sure!" Landon grabbed the disgusting object and dragged it toward the outside door.

"NO!" Brady suddenly blocked his path, voice shrill and face contorted.

"I'm taking it out because it's junk." Landon

tried to pass him.

Darica looked at Emelisa.  Would she intervene?

"NO!" Brady screamed again and launched himself against Landon with flailing fists and kicking feet.  Landon stumbled backward and plopped on the floor, losing his grip on the cat furniture.

Darica dashed to her brother's rescue, shoving Brady out of the way.  By the time Landon was on his feet again, Brady had dragged the piece of rubbish back to its corner.

Emelisa grimaced.  "Brady, we don't want it in here.  We told Landon to take it outside."

"NO!" Brady tore across the room and pummeled his sister in the stomach.

Emelisa grabbed her brother by both arms.  "Dad!" she shouted in a tone Darica had never heard her use before.  Brady writhed in his sister's grasp, aiming one foot and then the other at her knees.

Elwood appeared, swooped up Brady in a firm grasp, and carried him outside.  Angry screams of protest trailed behind them.

Darica and Danielle stood dumbfounded until Emelisa said, "Quick, get that thing out of sight before he comes back.  Sometimes he goes really crazy over something like that for no reason."

Landon looked uncertain, but Danielle exclaimed,

"Here comes the dumpster right now! We can throw this in and pile stuff on top, and Brady will never see it again." She grabbed one end while Landon took the other, and they disappeared out the door.

# NOTHING SO KINGLY

CHAPTER TEN

## Battlesome Brother

"This thing needs a slow-moving vehicle emblem on the back," Trevor muttered as he pushed the skid loader levers harder. "I should've walked. Brady will have the house torn down before I get there."

*Brady.* That was probably why he felt irritated about this project. Mom disliked trying to control Brady without Dad at home, which meant Trevor could never go anywhere alone with Dad. They always had to drag Brady along, and he usually caused enough trouble to make them all look like fools. It would be just like him to act up in front of Donovan's children.

*Bothersome brother.* The phrase popped into Trevor's mind from somewhere in the dim past. A reading story maybe? *Battlesome brother* would be a better name for Brady.

As Trevor jittered the skid loader onto Ridge Road, the little clapboard house came into view. He saw a waste removal truck chugging out the driveway, leaving a blue dumpster behind. If they had a dumpster to use, why did they need the skid loader? He wished Dad would have explained the plan to him.

Just then he saw Brady racing across the weedy yard, brandishing a stick. Who was he chasing? Danielle and Landon came tearing around the dumpster as if in danger of their lives.

Trevor steered the skid loader off the road and across the yard instead of taking time to reach the driveway. Jerking to a stop, he unbelted and leaped off. "Brady!" he yelled, running straight toward the little terrorist. "STOP!"

His tactic worked. Brady did not stop, of course, but he executed an amazing U-turn in attempt to flee from his brother. Trevor caught up, jerked the stick from Brady's hand, and shoved him to the ground. Brady set up an angry wail.

"Listen!" Trevor flopped down with an arm and leg across Brady to keep him from running away. "You can't chase people with a stick. They won't be your friends."

"I want that thing! I want it!" Brady gasped through his sobs.

Trevor felt footsteps and looked up to see Dad

coming across the yard.

"Now what?" Dad asked, as Trevor turned Brady over to him. "I was just out here a bit ago and thought I had him calmed down. Did you do something that got him going again?"

Fury rose in Trevor's chest, and his head pounded. Dad was blaming this on him? "I don't even know what happened before," he sputtered. "When I drove in, this boy was chasing Danielle and Landon with a stick. I had to stop him from hurting them. Why don't you just take him back where he belongs?"

Dad gave Trevor a hard look, and Trevor realized what Dad thought he meant. *He might as well be back in Romania*, he raged silently. "I mean he should have stayed at home," he said aloud. "Can't Mom take care of him so we can get something done?"

Ignoring the question, Dad said, "Bring the skid loader over to the back door of the lean-to. We'll load the trash on the bucket and haul it to the dumpster."

"I wanna do it!" Brady jerked wildly in Dad's grip.

Dad held on. "No, I'll drive. You may sit on my lap. Trevor, you can go in and take a look at what all needs to be thrown out the door."

Kicking aside tin cans, Trevor headed for the house. He opened the back door and stopped short. This was the worst mess he had ever seen!

Ceiling tile, cardboard boxes, and empty containers cluttered the floor. Water-stained insulation sagging from the ceiling contributed to the cave-like feeling. Trevor found himself hunkering down as if something might grab him. Several wall-mounted kitchen cabinets had surrendered their hold and lay splintered on the floor. Mold-covered dishes littered the countertop; greasy grime blackened the stove. Trevor shuddered.

The skid loader ground to a stop outside the door, and Brady burst in. "YUCK!" he screeched. "This is GROSS!"

Dad followed him with a shovel and a box of nitrile gloves. "Think we can make a difference here?" He raised his eyebrows at Trevor.

Trevor shrugged. He hadn't asked for the job, but he knew what Dad expected. Before he got one glove on, Brady had grabbed the shovel. "I'm a big bulldozer," he yelled, digging into the mess.

"Just push it out the door," Dad directed. "Right onto the skid loader bucket."

Trevor figured one scoopful would max Brady's tolerance, but to his surprise, the child kept at it. "Scoop the trash, dump the trash," he chanted as he shoved the conglomeration out the door. Dad and Trevor worked around him, sweeping trash off the countertop into empty boxes and hauling out the large chunks of insulation.

"Donovan is getting a crew lined up to replace this roof," Dad told Trevor. "After that, we'll put up a new ceiling in here."

"What about the cupboards?"

Dad tested a nearby cabinet door. "Rotten. The owner said he would pay for new ones if we finish pulling these down." He thumped against one of the cupboards under the counter top and peered inside. "I believe these are still sound. But we'll have to empty the junk out."

"Huh? What's in there?" Brady stuck his head under Dad's arm.

"More trash."

"I'll dig it out!"

Trevor couldn't believe his little brother's enthusiasm. Brady plowed head-first into a cupboard, and plastic bowls came flying out. Several kettles clattered to the floor as he explored the next cupboard. "Hey! It's all open inside here! See!" More doors flew open and more stuff flew out as Brady wiggled his way further inside. Soon he lay full length on the cupboard shelf. "See my new bunk bed," he shouted. "Trevor, you can sleep underneath me."

Trevor and Dad couldn't help laughing. For once they had found the right job for Brady.

# NOTHING SO KINGLY

CHAPTER ELEVEN

## To Play a Part

Church was over. Jolene listened enviously to Emelisa, Darica, and Danielle recounting their week. Apparently they had all spent several days working at the house for the new teacher's family.

Danielle turned to her. "You can't imagine how horrible it looked before we threw the trash out. But we have the worst part done now. I hope you can help us on cleaning day. We already scrubbed the walls once, but Daddy said there's no point in doing the final cleanup until they finish putting in new windows and ceiling tile."

"But we don't have much time left," Emelisa said. "Willis's family wants to move on Saturday. That's why Dad hired a remodeling crew to do some of the work."

"This Saturday?" Jolene asked.

"Yes, because that will give him just one week until school starts," Darica said. "He'll really have to scramble."

"Well, men teachers aren't that worried about decorations and stuff. Maybe he'll let us make the bulletin board display after school starts." Emelisa sounded hopeful.

"Yeah, that would be fun," Darica agreed.

Jolene felt her stomach tighten as it always did when her friends talked like this. With all their talents, they made life sound fun and easy. If only it could be that way for her, too. When Brother Willis saw Emelisa's lovely art work, he would despise Jolene's pitiful efforts.

As Jayden drove home from church, Jolene tried to think of a roundabout way to find out if she could help to clean Brother Willis's house. But the words kept tangling in her brain before she could utter them. Suddenly Mother's voice jolted her.

"Rosalie asked me to serve the meal for Willis's moving day. I offered that everyone could come to our house, but she said I should bring the food to Willis's, and we'll eat outside in the yard." Mother lowered her voice so that Jolene barely caught the last sentence. "I'd prefer to sit in air conditioning without flies buzzing around my food, but I guess some people are used to different things."

Jolene cracked her knuckles. Mother always talked as if no one else knew how to do things properly. But if Mother got to play a part in preparing for the new teacher, maybe she could, too. "The other girls have been helping to fix up Willis's house," she said. "Danielle hopes I can help them on cleaning day."

"I can't imagine why you would want to help with that!" Mother sounded disgusted. "We'll be busy enough getting the food ready."

Jolene chewed her lip to keep from retorting, "As if you'd let me help with *that*."

She spent Monday, Tuesday, and Wednesday hoping someone would call and ask for her help on cleaning day. But nobody did, at least not while she was in the house.

Mother fretted over the moving day menu, writing and rewriting lists in her planner. On Wednesday afternoon they went grocery shopping.

"I made two lists," she explained to Jolene on the way to the store, "one for each half of the store. We'll each take a cart and get the things on our list. Make sure you take a pen so you can cross things off as you put them into the cart. We can be efficient that way."

"That will be fun." Once in a while Mother surprised her with a privilege. "What all are we making?"

"Lasagna, lettuce salad, cheese balls and crackers, peach party dessert, and chocolate cream cheese bars."

"Sounds good." Jolene built a little secret hope in the corner of her mind: maybe Mother would let her bake the bars. She had made that recipe once before, and the bars had turned out okay.

At the store, Jolene took the list that consisted mostly of baking ingredients while Mother headed for the cold storage section. If she did this job carefully, maybe Mother would trust her with more important tasks. One by one, she crossed off the listed items, being careful to double check the number Mother had written after each one: *lasagna noodles—4, sugar—3, flour—3, crackers—2...*

When they met at the checkout, Mother took the list from Jolene and began to inventory her collection. Embarrassed, Jolene hurried to unload Mother's cart onto the checkout belt, hoping the cashier wouldn't notice that Mother didn't trust her.

The next morning while Jolene washed the breakfast dishes, Mother started cooking noodles and frying hamburger. Jolene carefully wiped the sinks and counter tops twice as Mother had taught her, while the question burned on her tongue.

When she hung up the dishcloth, she asked

hesitantly. "Do you think I could help make something—like the bars, maybe?"

Frowning, Mother considered her request. "I suppose you can try. Read the directions carefully and make only one recipe at a time. Double-check the ingredients as you go. Don't hurry or start daydreaming."

Jolene cringed, but she nodded dutifully. "Yes, I'll be careful. How many recipes shall I make?"

"Three."

Jolene found the recipe and took three packs of cream cheese from the refrigerator to soften. When she had mixed the chocolate batter for the first batch, she got out a cake pan and sprayed it with oil. Mother hovered over her shoulder. "Did you reread the list of ingredients?"

"Yes."

"I forgot to tell you to get the cream cheese out of the fridge."

"I remembered."

Mother said no more, but Jolene felt watched as she mixed the cream cheese filling, swirled it carefully into the chocolate batter, set the pan in the preheated oven, and pushed the timer buttons.

After repeating the process twice, she sighed with relief. Mother had another stack of dirty dishes ready for her to wash while the last batch baked, but Jolene didn't mind. At least she had been allowed to do one small deed for the new teacher.

# NOTHING SO KINGLY

CHAPTER TWELVE

## To Be Seen of Men

"Yeah! Do it again!" Megan and Othniel cheered as they stood beneath the swing set watching Everett skin the cat above their heads.

Everett flipped himself back up on the monkey bars, swung by his knees as long as he could, then hung by one hand before dropping to the ground.

"I'd be scared to drop that far." Megan's eyes shone with admiration.

"Do more tricks," Othniel begged.

Everett was climbing back up when Waylan startled him from behind. "It's time for you to come help me dig potatoes instead of doing things to be seen of men."

"Where'd you come from?"

"Helping Mom. Did you forget we're supposed to make sure she doesn't need to work so hard?"

Everett snooted. "Course not. Can't you see Megan and I hung out the laundry for her?" Waylan didn't need to think he was the only one who did his duty since Mom had been diagnosed with atrial fibrillation.

"Dad said as soon as we dig a bucketful of potatoes for Mom, we can go along to help with the moving."

"Serious?" Everett galloped toward the garden.

Twenty minutes later, Dad, Waylan, and Everett were driving to Brother Willis's place. Waylan asked, "How are we supposed to know what to do? It's been so long since anybody moved into the community that I almost forget."

"We helped Donovan's move in," Everett remembered.

"That was three years ago," Dad said. "Nathan and Joy got married since that, and their families helped them move in."

"Guess they didn't want anybody messing with their precious new stuff," Everett joked.

"Well, we want to be careful with anybody's possessions, new or not." Dad turned in Ridge Road. "The best way to help is to ask for instructions."

Trucks and vans filled the driveway and lawn at Willis's. People swarmed from the vehicles to the house, carrying boxes and furniture. Dad parked the pickup, and the boys trailed him to the back of the house where Donovan Wadel was coming out the door with an appliance cart.

"Good morning!" Donovan called out. "Glad to see you. Willis asked us to move the kitchen items in, but I need some man power to help with the heavy appliances."

Dad and Waylan followed Donovan up the ramp into the U-Haul. Assuming they didn't need him, Everett walked over to the van where Danielle and Landon were unloading boxes.

"Want to help us carry stuff to the basement? Landon asked.

"Sure." Everett stacked one box on top of another and hoisted them against his chest. "Whew! These are heavy!"

"Hey, those are glass jars," Danielle warned. "You'd better take one box at a time. The steps are kind of steep."

*Bossy girl!* Everett thought. But he remembered Dad's words about carefulness and Waylan's phrase about doing things to be seen of men. He set one box back down and followed Landon with the other one. Danielle was right about the steps.

"Okay, you boys can start unpacking jars and putting them on those shelves." Danielle pointed. "Cheryl said use one shelf for fruit and another for pickles. I'll bring the tomato juice down."

"This isn't very many jars," Landon said when the boxes were empty.

"Well, they just came back from Africa, so they don't have much yet." Everett flipped an empty box over his head and clenched his fingers into claws. "Here comes a big green monster..."

Landon yelled in pretend fright and jumped out of his way. Everett scrambled blindly in the direction of Landon's voice, sure that he could grab him.

"Stop!" screamed a girl's voice, but it was too late.

Everett crashed squarely into the person and something shattered on the floor. He whipped the box off his head and stood staring at Danielle.

She glared back at him, a mess of broken glass and tomato juice at her feet. "How could you do that to me?"

"I-I'm sorry," Everett stammered. "I didn't mean to. I'll clean it up."

"And you can tell Willis and Cheryl that it was your fault."

Everett hadn't known Danielle could get so mad. But he had done a foolish thing. He'd better go talk to Dad.

Before he found Dad, he met Brother Willis.

"Hello!" the new teacher greeted him. "I suppose you'll be one of my students?"

Everett nodded without meeting Willis's eyes. "I'm Everett," he mumbled. "But, um, I broke some jars in the basement, and, um, how should I clean it up?"

"Well, I'm not sure where the cleaning supplies are, but I'll go with you and see what we need."

Everett trailed behind Brother Willis, his face burning with shame. Danielle and Landon had disappeared. To Everett's amazement, four jars remained whole, apparently cushioned by the cardboard box Danielle had been carrying them in. He counted six broken ones with tomato juice puddled around them.

"Take the good ones over to the shelf," Brother Willis said. "There should be a bucket somewhere around here." He hurried over to the sink at the far end of the basement and returned with a three-gallon bucket and a rag. "I really need to go back upstairs. Use the bucket to carry the glass out to the dumpster and then get water from the sink to clean up the floor." He started for the inside basement stairs then turned to add, "Don't beat yourself up for the accident. Thanks for taking care of it."

Everett watched Willis's long legs disappear up the steps. Then he bent to his task. Would Brother Willis have been so kind if he had known what happened? He tried to console himself with the thought that he was taking all the blame; he wasn't making Danielle look bad. But why had he done such a foolish thing?

He was washing the floor when Danielle came down with another box. "That's the last of the jars," she said. "You can put them on the shelves. Jolene asked me to help set up for lunch." She dashed away before Everett could figure out whether she was still upset at him. Was she telling everybody what he had done? Slowly he finished arranging the jars. Maybe he could just stay in the basement while the others ate.

But Landon came looking for him. "Come on, Everett; lunch is ready."

"Where have you been all this time?" Waylan asked when they met on the lawn.

"Working in the basement." He waited tensely for Waylan's comments, but none came. The boys joined the lunch line behind Trevor.

"This yard used to look horrible," Waylan said. "Somebody must've worked hard, cleaning up the junk and mowing and trimming."

Trevor nodded.

"Did you help?"

"Yeah."

Emelisa walked past with a pitcher of water. "Don't let him fool you! He did the whole thing."

"Three cheers!" Waylan clapped Trevor on the shoulder.

To Everett's surprise, Trevor just shrugged off the praise.  No bragging or complaining, as he would have been tempted to do.

When it was their turn, the boys filled their trays and sat on the grass under the maple tree to eat.  The adults used the chairs that had been arranged nearby. Brother Willis was busy helping his little children with their food, but now and then Everett heard him make friendly remarks to his new acquaintances.

"This is a delicious lunch," the new teacher said to Jolene when the girls brought seconds around the circle. "I hear that your family provided it.  Thanks so much!"

"You're welcome."  Jolene's whisper barely reached Everett's ears.

"Did you make these scrumptious bars?" Cheryl asked her.

Jolene nodded, blushing.  Everett couldn't figure it out.  He loved compliments on the good stuff he baked.  These bars tasted super.  What did she have to be embarrassed about?  Maybe Waylan was right; he tried too hard to be seen of men. And then they ended up seeing him make foolish mistakes.  Well, he hoped he had grown up a little today, as Dad liked to say.

# Creekside School

| | |
|---|---|
| Lower Grade Teacher: | Sister Suzanne |
| Kindergarten: | Brady Kurtz (part time) |
| Grade 1: | Lashonda Wadel |
| | Jarrett Ebersole |
| | Megan Amstutz |
| Grade 2: | Cheyenne Brubaker |
| Grade 3: | Carlin Meyers |
| Grade 4: | Landon Wadel |
| | Quentin Amstutz |
| | |
| Upper Grade Teacher: | Brother Willis |
| Grade 6: | Everett Amstutz |
| Grade 7: | Danielle Wadel |
| | Jolene Ebersole |
| Grade 8: | Waylan Amstutz |
| | Emelisa Kurtz |
| Grade 9: | Darica Wadel |
| Grade 10: | Trevor Kurtz |

# NOTHING SO KINGLY

CHAPTER THIRTEEN

## Who Is Unrealistic?

The first day of school! Creek-scented breezes drifted through the open windows as Darica took her seat. She straightened the belt on her new rose dress and watched Brother Willis pace the front of the room. Footsteps clattered across the hardwood hall floor; Sister Suzanne's students were coming to join them for devotions.

Landon and Quentin came first. This was their fourth year of sitting on the little chairs lined up along the chalkboard at the side of the room. Carlin followed, walking stiffly and looking neither to the right hand nor to the left. Darica always felt sorry for Carlin. He was the only child in his family as well as the only one in his grade. He needed someone to bring him to life.

Brother Willis's Cheyenne came next. *Spritely*

was the word to describe her, Darica thought. Even though it was her first day at a new school, she didn't act scared. But why should she be, with her daddy here, too?

Now the first graders were straggling in, looking at everything on the way. Megan paused beside Everett's desk, and Lashonda bumped into her. By the time Megan had figured out where to sit, Lashonda had stopped to gape at the "Welcome Back" bulletin board. Darica frowned. Where was Sister Suzanne? Should she get up and direct her little sister to a chair?

At last Sister Suzanne came through the doorway, leading an unwilling Jarrett with tearstained cheeks. She seated him on the chair nearest her own, then reached over to guide the girls to their places. Darica figured it was a good thing Brady wasn't here today, too. On the way to school, she had told Lashonda about devotions, but she must not have been paying attention.

Brother Willis welcomed the group to a new school year and led the song "We'll Follow with Rejoicing." Lashonda's shrill little voice rang out, some of her words half a syllable early, and Darica felt her face redden. Why couldn't her little sister blend with the others? She had tried so hard to teach her to sing nicely in preparation for school. In fact, she had purposefully helped her siblings memorize some of their favorite school songs, because she hated to see the younger ones gaping and wriggling while the older ones sang. With fewer than two dozen people singing together, everyone had to do their part. But Lashonda was overdoing it, and on the first day at that!

Darica felt relieved when devotions ended, and the younger children returned to their own class-room. But alas, the first thing on Brother Willis's agenda was math class. Darica looked at Emelisa and wrinkled her nose as he passed out speed drill papers. The two of them had long agreed that math was the hardest subject, and whoever heard of having it first thing in the day? Brother Mose had always started with English or literature.

"Let's sharpen our brains by trying to do one hundred number facts in a minute," Brother Willis said. "I'll join you, because I'm afraid my brain got rusty over summer, too. If you finish before my timer beeps, stand up. If you don't, just stop wherever you are."

*Unrealistic!* Darica fumed. *Nobody can do more than one problem per second.* Then she saw the look on Waylan's face and knew that he was determined to beat the timer. Well, she would give it all she had.

"Ready, set, go!" Brother Willis called out.

Heads bent.  Pencils scratched.

The word *staccato* popped into Darica's mind, but she pushed it aside to concentrate on elusive numbers.  End of first row.  End of second.

On her seventh row, Trevor stood up. Eighth row, Waylan bounced to his feet.  Halfway through the tenth row, Emelisa stood.  Darica's heart pounded.  She scribbled frantically.  She was writing the first digit of her last answer when the timer beeped.

Disgusting!  She never had been able to equal Trevor's math skills, but to have the eighth graders beat her as well hurt Darica's pride.  If Brother Willis kept this up, she would have to do some extra practice at home.

Before she recovered from the speed drill trauma, Brother Willis announced that Darica and Trevor would study algebra together.  Darica clenched her fists in desperation until she remembered that Daddy was an algebra expert.  A life jacket to keep her from drowning!

When Brother Willis dismissed them for the 10:00 intermission, he pointed out that he had narrowed the recess down to ten minutes instead of the twenty minutes Brother Mose had always allowed. This would enable them to fit all the English and reading classes into the schedule without shortening lunch time.

"That's not enough time for a volleyball game," Trevor muttered as the others followed him outside.

"King's Base then," Waylan said. "Everybody grab a base."

English classes came next. Brother Willis handed out quizzes to assess his students' knowledge. After Darica labeled each word in a compound complex sentence with the correct part of speech and diagrammed it without a mistake, Brother Willis said she might as well join Trevor in the tenth grade English course so that he wouldn't have to teach two individual classes. Darica smiled. No worries about Trevor outdoing her in English.

Since she had done ninth-grade literature with Trevor the year before, Brother Willis assigned her to work through the eighth-grade book with Emelisa and Waylan. Darica was glad; she hadn't wanted to miss those stories.

After lunch, Brother Willis brought out a stack of brand-new science books. "I understand that none of you have used any of this science curriculum before, so I decided to have you all work through the seventh-grade book, at least for the first half of this year. We can enjoy the discussions and demonstrations together that way."

Darica glanced at Emelisa, who raised her eyebrows in return. What kind of sense did it make for her and Trevor to do the same assignments as Everett, Jolene, and Danielle? But the new teacher didn't seem to care what they thought. He enthusiastically handed out the books and introduced the first unit. As Darica opened her book and breathed in the smell of fresh ink, she managed to shove aside her doubts and feel some of Brother Willis's enthusiasm.

Music class brought the biggest shock of the day. Brother Willis passed out pieces of scrap paper and instructed each student to each write which part he or she preferred to sing. Then he collected the slips and laid them out in a row on his desk. After a moment, he said, "Well, it looks as if we have some work to do! I know there are just a few of us, but I hope we can learn to sing in four parts."

Darica glanced around at her classmates. She guessed that most of them had written *soprano*. Brother Mose had no aptitude for singing, so music class had never been on his schedule. Trevor had learned to sing tenor, probably at home or church, but last year Waylan and Everett had still sung soprano, their voices unchanged.

Next, Brother Willis passed out music workbooks. Darica hadn't known such a thing existed.

She flipped through hers and saw dozens of unfamiliar terms and symbols. How in the world did their teacher expect them to jump into stuff they had never heard of before?

Play time posed another problem. Brother Willis had scheduled their afternoon recess to begin ten minutes before the lower grade recess ended.

"How can we play softball when they're playing kickball?" Waylan voiced the upper graders' mutual dismay as they burst out into the sunshine.

"Sister Suzanne and I talked about this earlier," Brother Willis answered. "Our class will join their kickball game until their recess ends. The younger children can learn from you, and more players will make the game go better. Waylan's team can be in first, and Trevor's team outfield."

"Huh!" Trevor snorted in disgust and smacked the softball hard into his glove.

Darica knew how he felt. But he could be glad Brady wasn't here today. Dealing with younger siblings' inabilities was the most embarrassing part of a small school. Sure enough, as they walked onto the ball diamond, Lashonda tried so valiantly to kick the red rubber ball that she tumbled to the ground and landed right on top of it.

Darica ran to help her up. "Stand here. Like this."

She moved Lashonda into position. "Now kick!" she yelled as Sister Suzanne sent the ball rolling along the ground.

Lashonda connected, and the ball rolled half-way to the pitcher's mound. She stood watching as Megan picked it up.

"Run!" Darica pointed to first base. "Quick, or Megan will catch you!"

"Run, Megan! Get her!" Everett shouted at his sister.

Neither first grader seemed to understand. They stood looking at each other and giggling until Darica towed Lashonda to first base.

By the end of the day, Darica felt tangled up. Part of her wanted to accept Brother Willis, but the rest of her felt disgruntled with the new ideas he was imposing on their school. At home in their bedroom, she grumbled to Danielle, "I wish every-thing would stay like it was before."

Danielle yanked off her socks. "I thought you were tired of Brother Mose."

"I was." Darica grabbed her barn dress from the closet. "But I didn't say Brother Willis had to completely revise our school system."

Daddy met them in the milking parlor. "How was the first day?"

"I think we're going to have an interesting year!" Danielle started filling dippers.

"If Brother Willis doesn't get too unrealistic." Darica jerked unit washers off the milkers with more force than necessary.

Daddy looked surprised. "You don't like him?"

"He's okay," Darica amended. "He just has some different ideas."

"I already know he's completely different from Brother Mose, but why did you say 'unrealistic'?"

"Probably because we're all having science together," Danielle said.

Daddy grinned. "You can blame that on me. When Brother Willis asked at board meeting about using a new science curriculum instead of the outdated books we had before, I suggested a trial run of one grade level to see if we liked them before spending for the whole set. We thought the assignments looked a little tougher than the old books anyway." He looked at Darica. "I thought you and Trevor had enough hard subjects that you wouldn't mind an easy one."

Darica nodded. "We have to do algebra and tenth grade English. And you ought to see the horrible music books he came up with! We don't know a thing about that stuff, because Brother Mose never taught us one iota of music!"

"I'm sorry he didn't. But Brother Willis helped to write these new music workbooks, and believe me, he knows the material. He's really into music and wants to teach it thoroughly. I think you'll enjoy it." Daddy looked Darica straight in the eyes, and she saw a twinkle. "I thought you were the smart girl who likes challenges, looks up new words, and teaches everybody else—"

Darica sighed. "Okay, I'll do my best to handle it. But the thing I'm really unimpressed with is teaching the little youngsters how to play ball. Lashonda made such a fool of herself!" She launched into a detailed description of her little sister's actions.

Daddy nodded understandingly, but he was smiling when she finished. "Now who is unrealistic?" he asked. "You think Brother Willis is expecting a lot of you as his new student, but aren't you expecting a lot of Lashonda as a first grader? I know you worked hard to prepare her for school, and that was helpful of you, but you still need to let her be the first grader that she is. She can't learn everything in one day, and everybody knows that. It's no discredit to you if she makes some blunders. See what I mean?"

"Uh-huh." Darica could follow Daddy's logic. But she couldn't resist one more comment. "Since it truly is unrealistic to expect me to do algebra without making blunders, you'll have to teach me the tricks."

"Sure," Daddy said. "After you get the cows milked."

# NOTHING SO KINGLY

## CHAPTER FOURTEEN

## Trevor's Trials

Trevor plowed through another verse of "Nobil-ity." These poems in his literature book! He had never liked poetry to start with, and this one rambled about what he had missed in life—which was plenty, in his opinion.

> "We cannot make bargains for blisses,
>    Nor catch them like fishes in nets;
> And sometimes the thing our life misses
>    Helps more than the thing which it gets.
> For good lieth not in pursuing,
>    Nor gaining of great nor of small,
> But just in the doing, and doing
>    As we would be done by, is all."

Ignoring the rest of the poem, Trevor propped his

chin on his fist and surveyed the stuffy classroom from his seat at the back of the middle row. In front of him, the curly ends of Darica's braids brushed her chair back as she bent over a spiral bound tablet, writing as if her life depended on it. How could she have finished her algebra lesson already?

Jolene sat in front of Darica, flipping listlessly through her science book. Trevor shook his head. That girl would never make sense of anything scientific. She gave such embarrassing answers in class.

On Trevor's left, Everett propped his elbow on his reader and spun his ruler on the end of a pencil. Brother Willis had just dismissed the sixth and seventh grade reading class, and the lunch bell would ring in half a minute. In front of Everett, Danielle sat on one foot, redeeming the time by reading the next story.

Emelisa and Waylan made up the row on Trevor's right. Waylan, who always buzzed through his work without concern for perfection, was reading *Haunt Fox* while Emelisa wrote long, flourishing answers to her history questions.

They were all nice enough classmates, but what Trevor needed was another boy in ninth or tenth grade, someone who wanted to talk about ideas instead of just chit-chat. The Amstutz boys and the Wadel girls discussed farming details, but he couldn't relate to that. They gabbed about the funny things their little siblings did, but none of them had a brother as bad as Brady. This morning Emelisa had kept quiet during such a discussion, and Trevor had guessed that she was just as stressed as he was about Brady's first kindergarten day.

How would Brother Willis relate to Brady? The new teacher wasn't harsh, although Trevor could tell he held higher expectations for his students than Brother Mose had. He was almost too particular; he rarely digressed into storytelling or discussions of the sort Brother Mose had liked.

The lunch bell rang. After prayer, the seven students promptly washed their hands and sat down with their lunchboxes.

Everett started talking with his sandwich halfway to his mouth. "Darica, what are you all the time writing in your tablet?"

Darica grinned and tossed her braids. "Words."

Danielle swiveled her chair. "She writes stories."

Everett took a big bite and asked around it, "Gonna write a book?"

"Probably sometime." Darica tried to sound modest.

"That'd be neat," Waylan joined in. "When I write a book, I'll make it turn out wrong. I don't like how books always end so perfect."

"What's the story you're writing now?" Emelisa asked Darica.

"*Katie's Canal Boat*.   Like on the school trip, remember?"

Emelisa nodded.

"It's a terribly good story," Danielle bragged. "She told it to us all summer."

Trevor wondered later why he said it, but at the moment he just had to interject something into this silly discussion.  "When I write a book, I'm going to call it *Zero, No Brain at All*."

His classmates laughed appreciatively, except Jolene.  Trevor wondered if he had offended her.

"I guess it'll be about people who do crazy stuff," Waylan said.

"I'd have plenty of material," Trevor muttered, recognizing a certain loud voice from Sister Suzanne's room.

A few minutes later, Sister Suzanne stepped into the hallway between the two classrooms.  She motioned for Emelisa to come.  Emelisa raised her eyebrows at Trevor and went.

Trevor's stomach twisted, and he dropped his chips back into his lunchbox.  It had to be a problem with Brady.

When Emelisa returned, she leaned across the aisle and mouthed to Trevor, "She said he won't eat anything. I told her that's normal; don't worry about it."

Trevor nodded, relieved. Not a big problem after all. Mom should have remembered to tell Sister Suzanne that Brady rarely ate in a strange environment.

After lunch, Brother Willis started science class with a quiz on the vocabulary they had learned so far: *experiment, hypothesis, data...* Trevor sighed. This was the boring part of science—just talking about what it was. He had studied this before, even though he hadn't done this book. But after they had discussed the quiz and homework answers, Brother Willis presented a new idea.

"As soon as we finish this short introductory unit, I'm planning to skip to Unit Three and study light while we still have warm, sunny days. When you boys have spare time, please read ahead in that unit and figure out what we'll need for setting up demonstrations. You can help me collect lenses and figure out where we can project images best."

Project images? That sounded challenging. Trevor's spirit lifted a little. This would give him some common ground with the younger boys, something interesting to discuss and work on together. He would be the undisputed leader, but they would make great sidekicks.

Recess time came, and Trevor's distress returned. Now everybody in his room would come face to face with his brother's incongruities. He had managed to teach Brady how to kick a ball, but nobody could ever persuade him to take turns.

Outside, Trevor saw immediately that the ball diamond was empty. The little children were playing link tag on the driveway. He inwardly blessed Sister Suzanne for her good judgment. But as soon as Brady saw the upper graders, he lost interest in his own playmates and dropped out of the line. He wandered over to the edge of the grass and stood watching until Sister Suzanne called him back.

Trevor took his place on the pitcher's mound and sent a fast ball to Waylan who hit it on the first crack. It soared upward, a lovely pop. Brother Willis dashed in from the outfield to catch it at the same moment that Brady came tearing across the yard to get away from Landon and Cheyenne. Brother Willis's head was up, his eyes on the ball. No one could yell soon enough to prevent the catastrophe, but most of them screamed as Brother Willis landed on top of Brady. Brady howled as if he were being dismembered.

Mortified, Trevor watched his teacher untangle

himself and lift the flailing child to his feet. Sister Suzanne hurried over, took Brady by the hand, and apologized for the interference. As she led him away, Trevor saw her motioning as if to point out the boundaries of each game. He guessed that she had told Brady before, but it hadn't made a dent on his hard skull. That boy would manage to spoil the school year for everybody. The thought left Trevor with no ambition for the ball game.

# NOTHING SO KINGLY

CHAPTER FIFTEEN

## What's Wrong with Us?

Jolene opened her lunch box and stared at the contents. One yogurt cup. One pack of pretzel sticks with cheese dip. No juice. No fruit. She clenched her jaw and cracked her knuckles to keep from crying.

It had been another bad morning. She glanced at her classmates from the corners of her eyes. What if they could guess by seeing her lunch how Mother acted sometimes? In spite of the late summer heat in the classroom, goosebumps rose on Jolene's arms. It was scary, never being sure if it was Mother's mind or her own that was off track.

Why did Mother sometimes tell her she looked just fine and could eat whatever she liked, but the next time she couldn't stop fussing about healthful food? Usually Jolene was supposed to pack her own lunch; this morning Mother had taken over, declaring that Jolene had been eating too much. But it was Mother who bought junk food; Jolene preferred ham sandwiches and fresh fruit over this packaged stuff.

"Jolene! Hey, Jolene!" Danielle waved her napkin. "Can you come?

"Where?" Jolene asked. Oh, why couldn't she break this habit of blocking out the conversation around her? It got her into such predicaments.

"To our house on Friday evening," Danielle explained. "To work on the bulletin board."

So, they must have been planning a get-together to work on the room decorations. She would feel like a dunce at that. But at least they were inviting her. Then she remembered. The family gathering. The horrible Saunders gathering. Her family was invited to *that* on Friday evening.

"I-I can't." She fumbled with the pretzel pack in her lunch box. "We have to go to family gathering."

"We can wait until some other time," Darica offered from behind her.

Jolene turned and saw Darica eating red cinnamon apple salad; it smelled delicious. "I don't care. You can do it without me."

"Could we do it on Saturday?" Emelisa suggested.

Darica shook her head. "Doubt if Mom would

like that. She always has plenty of work for us on Saturday morning."

"And we all take naps in the afternoon." Danielle opened her container of apple salad.

Darica wrinkled her nose. "I guess you think we sound like babies, but we have to get up to milk at 4:30 in the morning, and Daddy hates to see us sleep in church."

"That's okay. Each family has to do what works for them." Emelisa popped a grape into her mouth.

Jolene's thoughts drifted again. She knew their family had some unusual ways of doing things. But those things didn't really work so well. So why did they do them? She guessed it was because of Mother's family being so odd. She shivered again at the thought of the family gathering. Why did Mother want to go?

Friday evening came too quickly. Mother gave rapid instructions on the way home from school.

"Change your clothes and feed the dogs immediately," she told Jolene. "Don't poke around petting them. Then I need you to wash dishes. I'm almost finished frosting the cupcakes."

Jolene wondered why Mother hadn't finished the cupcakes before, but she didn't ask. Mother always got up tight about doing things with her family —

they dare not be late, the food had to be perfect, the children needed to do exactly what she wanted.

Jolene did her best to please Mother, and by the time Father and Jayden came from the shop, she and Jarrett had finished their chores and dressed according to Mother's specifics. Jolene doubted that her girl cousins who wore all sorts of store-bought clothing would care whether she wore a pink flowered dress or a blue striped one, but Mother seemed to think they would be more impressed with the pink one.

An hour later, Jolene sat at one of the tables in Grandpa's basement, trying to act hungry for the over-abundant selection of food. On her left, Macy chatted with one of their boy cousins about her newest video game. To her right, Aunt Rochelle was engrossed in her boyfriend, a fellow with long sideburns and ear pins. Jolene supposed her aunt had met him at school.

As she slowly chewed her ham sandwich, Jolene looked at her grandparents who were seated at the head of the table. Grandpa was bald, red-faced, and saggy-bellied. He had not been a Christian or a church-goer for years and years. But Jolene remembered how shocked she had felt the day Jayden told her that Grandpa drank liquor.

"You mean he actually gets drunk?"

"Of course. That's why he doesn't have license sometimes, and Grandma has to haul him around."

Grandma wore a tiny covering and went to church when her arthritis wasn't too bad. Jolene could hardly imagine a time when Grandma had dressed like Mother did now, but she had seen pictures to prove it. In his twenties, Grandpa had come from the world and joined a conservative church where he met and married Grandma. When his drinking problem came to light, he was excommunicated. Mother never talked about Grandpa's problems, but Father had explained to Jolene what had happened.

Grandma had taken her children to the same church for several years before changing to a more liberal church that she thought would win Grandpa's favor. Mother, the oldest, had been thirteen by then and unwilling to leave her friends. She had convinced Grandma to let her go to church with Grandma's parents, and that was how she had married Father.

As Grandpa and Grandma tried various churches, their other six children stopped off at different points along the way. Looking around at her relatives, Jolene counted at least four different church groups besides the one her family was part of. Aunt Rochelle had never joined any church at all. She cut her hair and wore jeans. Grandpa's television had always been available to her, and she had chosen to attend public high school.

"Hey, Jo!" Macy interrupted her thoughts. "What've you been doing with yourself?"

"Um, nothing much. Just going to school, mostly. We have a new teacher this year."

"Is he cool?"

Jolene cracked her knuckles under the table. What was she supposed to say? A teacher was a teacher to her—someone who made her do lessons. "He's okay."

"Does he do videos?"

"No."

"My teacher does. He's really into sports, and he uses videos to show us advanced techniques in soccer and volley ball. We get to do some on-line stuff this year, and that's pretty neat."

"Yeah, we do, too," another cousin joined in.

They jabbered on in terminology that Jolene did not recognize. She shut them out and wondered again why her family had to be so different. She didn't fit in anywhere. Did Mother feel that way, too? Jolene wished they could have stayed at home.

# NOTHING SO KINGLY

## CHAPTER SIXTEEN

## Too Many Irons in the Fire

"Did you find that old pair of binoculars you were talking about?" Trevor asked Waylan as they headed for the ball diamond.

"Yes, Dad said I can do whatever with them, since they don't work right anymore."

"Can you tear them apart tonight so we can use those lenses tomorrow?"

"Sure."

"What about the periscope?"

Waylan turned to Everett. "Did you get the stuff all collected for that?"

"I don't know how to cut the mirrors to the right size." Everett looked hopefully at the older boys for suggestions.

"Stephanie could do that for you," Trevor offered. "She cuts glass to make mottos. How about if you bring everything along tomorrow?"

Waylan and Everett nodded. "We should be able to get a lot of stuff ready tonight."

When school dismissed, the Amstutz children found Gary in the driver's seat of their van. Othniel and Cordell yelled enthusiastic greetings from their car seats.

"What's the deal?" Waylan jumped in beside Cordell who grabbed his arm in a tight hug. Usually if Mom couldn't come for them, she kept the little children at home with her.

Gary explained, "Mom was having atrial fibs, so Dad took her to the hospital."

"Didn't they come back yet?" Megan wailed.

"I don't know. They might be home when we get there."

But they weren't. Waylan carried Cordell into the kitchen and saw a pile of dishes in the sink.

Megan's tears flowed. "I want Mom. Who's going to make supper?"

Waylan looked at Everett. "We can have hotdogs, can't we?"

Everett nodded. "If I can find some in the freezer.

"Get them out to thaw. And some buns, too," Gary said. "One of you can take care of the children, and the other should come to the barn.

Roger's out there scraping barnyard."

"I want to go out." Othniel yanked on Gary's arm.

"That works," Waylan said. "Quentin can help us feed calves. Everett can stay in here with Megan and Cordell."

"Can't you call Mom?" Megan begged.

Gary opened the plastic container on the countertop and handed out cookies. "I'll call Dad while you all go change clothes."

"They're still in the ER," he reported when his siblings came back downstairs. "Dad thinks they'll probably keep Mom overnight and see if changing her medication helps. He says just do the chores and keep our boat floating the best we can."

Waylan showed Quentin and Othniel which calf pens needed fresh straw. Then he went to help Gary. When they had all sixteen milkers attached, he carried milk to the calf barn and told the younger boys how to measure out the grain. Back and forth he ran all evening, helping here and managing there.

"I feel like an old pappy," he groaned to Gary. "Can't Roger come in here and help you soon?"

"He's running out feed to the cows right now, so he should be around soon. But, hey, you're doing great! Thanks for being so responsible."

Waylan grinned. It felt good to be praised by his

older brother. That was the reason he preferred Gary above Roger, who tended to be grumpy and fault-finding. Momentarily he remembered Trevor's request for the science demonstration items. When would he and Everett find time for that?

When the boys finally reached the house at 7:30, Waylan immediately noticed a Jetta parked in the driveway. "Hey, look!" he whooped. "Aunt Phyllis!"

"Lucky for us!" Roger said. "We won't have to do women's work."

Aunt Phyllis, Dad's single sister, managed a bakery, but she was never too busy to drive an hour if her relatives were in need. She had been a favorite of the Amstutz children since their babyhood.

"See our good supper!" Megan jumped up and down as her brothers entered the kitchen. "Aunt Phyllis brought subs and whoopie pies from her bakery."

Everett looked equally happy. "I didn't have to cook hotdogs!"

"Did Dad call you?" Gary asked his aunt.

She nodded. "I told my employees I wouldn't be in until eleven tomorrow, so I can stay overnight and help you get everybody around for school in the morning."

"She's going to sleep with me!" Megan bounced around the table.

"That's good." Waylan knew how hard it was for

Megan to go to bed alone when Mom wasn't around.

By the time they had finished supper, the little children were falling asleep. Waylan and Everett carried
them up to their beds. Just when Waylan thought
they were peacefully settled, Cordell began to
cry, "Mommy, Mommy."

Waylan wrapped him in his fuzzy blanket and
sat down on the floor to rock him. "Mommy's
sick. Waylan will take care of you." He sang softly,
"Twinkle, twinkle, little star..."

"Shall I get him some milk?" Everett whispered
when Cordell continued to fuss.

"Yes, and tell Quentin to take his bath."

While Cordell sucked his sippy cup, Waylan worried about Mom. What if she had a heart attack and
needed surgery? What if the doctors couldn't fix her
problem and she... He cut the thought short. God
wouldn't take away the mother of eight children,
would He? He wished Dad would come home, so
he could hear with his own ears what was going on.
As it was, he had to take everything through Gary.
Not that Gary was mean about telling him, but he
was afraid to let Gary know how anxious he was.

When Cordell finally fell into a deep sleep, the
other boys in the room were already snoring.
Waylan stretched his weary back a moment and

contemplated going to talk with Gary. But his
eyes ached and the thought of morning chores
sent him tumbling into bed.

In the morning, Dad called to say that since
Mom's heart monitor had shown no irregularities
during the night, the doctor said he would dis-
charge her before noon. Aunt Phyllis volunteered
to stay until they got home. That cheered the little
ones who had cried with disappointment to find
Mom still missing when they woke. Megan fussed
about needing to go to school, but Aunt Phyllis
solved that by helping her pack a special lunch.

Not until they were on the way to school did
Waylan remember his promise to Trevor. "Everett,
we forgot the binoculars and mirrors for science!"

Everett wrinkled his face. "Gary, can you bring
it for us?"

"What?" Gary hadn't been paying attention to
their conversation.

"Our science stuff. It's on the table in Mom's
sewing room, so the little children don't mess with
it. I ran out of time last night, but if you bring it
to school for me—"

Gary was shaking his head before Waylan finished explaining. "Sorry, but I have too many irons
in the fire to make an extra trip to school. Dad's

been wanting Roger and me to clean out the dry cow and heifer pens and move animals around while it's nice out. And the combine will probably come, which means we'll have corn to haul to the mill."

Waylan sighed. Would "too many irons in the fire" be a good enough excuse to pacify Trevor?

# NOTHING SO KINGLY

CHAPTER SEVENTEEN

## Fact or Fiction?

D arica shook her head in disgust as she shoved the algebra book inside her desk. It didn't make enough sense to waste lead on. Three of her equations hadn't come out equal; she'd take those home and get Daddy's help. Pulling out her assignment book, she checked off algebra, English, and literature. Music yet. That was as bad as algebra; she'd take it home, too.

She checked the clock. Good, only three minutes until time to go help Sister Suzanne. Monday, Wednesday, and Friday were her days; Tuesday and Thursday were Emelisa's. Darica pulled out her tablet and added a few sentences to her story until she saw Sister Suzanne open her door and send Lashonda out to the hall.

Darica hopped up and headed out to meet her

little sister with a smile. They sat down at the hall table, and Lashonda opened her word practice book.

"These word helpers are easy-peasy," she declared. "You won't have to stop me one time!"

"Okay, let's go." Darica slid the bookmark under sa.

Lashonda read down the column without a snag.

"Great job," Darica praised her.

"You know what?" Lashonda leaned close. "Megan was crying, and she can't say her sounds."

"Megan? Oh, is it because her mommy is in the hospital?"

Lashonda shrugged. "I don't know. Is she?"

"Yes, she's having heart problems again. Waylan and Everett were talking about it."

"Will she die?"

"I don't think so. The doctors will give her medicine. Now read the rest of your page, so you can go back to your work."

Jarrett came out next. *Tedious* was the word for him, Darica thought as he struggled to form the sounds. Would Megan be able to do any better? Poor little girl, she must be so stressed about her mom. And suddenly, Darica knew what would happen next in her story. Katie's mom would get deathly sick—yes, she would actually die—and Katie would need to deal with her siblings' reactions. It would be a tale of pathos and tears. In the midst of it all, Katie would need someone to comfort her—

"I'm done. Hey, I'm done!" Jarrett jostled against her chair.

"Oh!" Darica came back to real life and moved the bookmark to the next column.

By the time Jarrett had finished his page, Darica had planned another installment of "Katie's Canal Boat." She waited for Megan to appear, wondering what she should do if the child burst into inconsolable sobs.

But Megan read without a tear. Then she closed her book and whispered, "My mommy's in the hospital."

"I hope she gets better soon," Darica sympathized.

Megan nodded and hopped off her chair. "She's going to." She smiled at Darica as she turned to go. "Aunt Phyllis slept with me last night."

Darica smiled back and marked it down as a six-year-old's reaction for her story.

Back in her own desk, Darica snatched out her tablet and began to write about Katie's mother's deathly illness. What should it be? Malaria? Typhoid fever? Dysentery? Better do some research to see which one would work best. She hurried to the encyclopedia shelf and selected several volumes. Back at her seat, she flipped to typhoid and began to read.

"Darica."

She jumped at the sound of Brother Willis's voice. "Are you finished your assignments?"

Flustered, she gave a quick nod, wondering if she should have asked permission to use the encyclopedia.

"Then you and Emelisa may help Trevor and Waylan set up the science demonstration." He turned back to the sixth and seventh grade social studies class.

As Darica put her things away, a sudden hot feeling swept over her. Had she told a lie about her assignments if she planned to take her algebra and music home? She shoved the thought aside and went to join her classmates at the science table.

"Where are those binocular lenses?" Trevor was asking Waylan.

"I'm sorry," Waylan said, "but we just didn't have time for anything like that last night. With Dad and Mom away, and all the chores to do..."

Darica hoped Trevor would say something forgiving, but instead he grimaced and said, "Well, let's figure out if we have all the stuff for any of these other demos."

It seemed that nobody else's heart was in the project any more than hers was. When Brother

Willis called them to class five minutes later, Trevor reported dryly, "Project on hold until next shipment arrives."

"Sounds like a mini barn builder!" Brother Willis grinned. "We have plenty to discuss, so let's go ahead with the lesson."

"Tell me what you wrote about Katie's family today," Danielle begged that evening in the milking parlor.

"I didn't have time to plan it all yet. Why does everybody have to keep pushing everybody else?"

Danielle raised her eyebrows. "Sorry, didn't mean to make you mad."

Darica turned her face away and wiped cows furiously for a few minutes. She had been worrying about whether Brother Willis had noticed her sneaking her algebra and music lessons home and what she would say if he accused her of lying to him.

"It's really tough for Megan that Mabel is in the hospital," she said finally. "And for the boys, too. Trevor wasn't very nice to Waylan about not bringing the science stuff. I felt sorry for them."

Danielle nodded. "Mom said Mabel did get home today, so everything should go better for them tonight."

Darica struggled to push aside the thought

of her unfinished assignments and jump into her imaginary world with Katie, but somehow the usual pleasure had disappeared.

# NOTHING SO KINGLY

CHAPTER EIGHTEEN

## Brady's Backpack

Stephanie came to drive Trevor and Emelisa home from school. "Mom and Brady went along with Dad to deliver a mini barn," she explained.

Trevor made no response. What did it matter? He would work alone as usual, and they would all be back soon enough.

"How was your day?" Stephanie asked.

Emelisa obliged her by giving some details, but Trevor shut them both out. Today didn't have any bragging points, and tomorrow would be horrible—a Brady day at school.

Out in the shop, Trevor pounded nails furiously. Of all the students in the upper grade room, his life was the worst. Yeah, he knew he should feel sorry for Waylan and Everett worrying about their mom in the hospital, but what was the big deal about their chores?  With all those brothers...

"How are you doing?" Dad's voice made Trevor jump.

Before he could answer, Brady marched in, swinging a ball bat.  He whacked the first board pile he met, thumped the concrete floor all the way to the next one, struck it, and came over to beat on the frame Trevor was building.

Dad ignored him and headed for the office. Trevor boiled.  If Dad couldn't control this brat, he would. "Stop it!" he commanded.

Brady swung the bat at him.  Trevor grabbed it mid-swing.  Brady screamed.

Dad turned around and came back, frowning at Trevor.  "Why can't you leave him alone?"

"Why can't he leave *me* alone?" Trevor retorted. "Beating me and my building with his dumb bat just because I'm out here slaving away when you get home from running around—I'm sick of such shines."

"Trevor!"

Trevor grabbed another board and began pounding nails.  He knew without looking what kind of expression went with that tone of voice.  He knew what kind of lecture Dad was gearing up to give him, and he was not going to listen to it *one more time*.

By now, Brady had jumped on his bike and was

tearing around the shop, the ball bat forgotten.

"What's wrong that you and Brady can't get along anymore?" Dad asked.

"He messes up my whole life." Trevor slammed his hammer down and missed the nail. "Now he's ruining our family's reputation at school, too." He knew better than to talk like this to Dad, but right now he was too angry to stop himself. "Why did you adopt him anyway? Because I wasn't a good enough son for you? Because you didn't—"

"Stop!" Dad interrupted. "No more talk like that. You know why we adopted Brady. We heard about orphans in Romania who needed homes. Mom always wished for more children, especially a brother for you, and it seemed this was God's way of granting that desire. Now you're saying you don't appreciate the gift you have been given? Of course, Brady has his problems. You would too, if you had had such a rough start in life—"

Trevor blocked the rest. Dad always pitied poor little Brady and excused him at the expense of his own flesh-and-blood son. It made no sense at all.

Morning came, and Trevor considered staying in bed rather than getting up to face a Brady school day. But that would only create more issues in the family. Sure enough, as soon as he opened his bedroom door, he heard Brady's angry voice hurling insults at Mom.

"The school clothes problem again," Emelisa said, dragging a hamper full of laundry from the bathroom.

Trevor grimaced.  Brady hated wearing socks. His favorite shirt was a thread-bare everyday one. His choice pair of pants had holes in both knees. Judging by his howls, putting on decent clothing was as painful as getting splinters removed.

"They scratch!" he yelled. "I want soft ones. Mom, buttons are stupid! NO! Don't want socks!"

Emelisa brought a handful of clothes hangers from her bedroom closet. "Mom and Sister Suzanne think the school routine is good for Brady, so after Christmas he'll probably go three times a week."

"Oh, help!" Trevor sagged against the hall wall. "That'll be the end of me.  Hey, I thought Sister Suzanne was too busy for more time with Brady."

"She said we girls might need to help her more.  I guess I'll have to take Brady, because Darica already complains about how ignorant Jarrett is compared to Lashonda.  I don't think she'd have the patience to deal with Brady."

"She prefers perfect people, huh?" Trevor snorted.

Emelisa put a finger to her lips in warning.  Brady

came charging up the stairs with Mom following.

"I'm getting it; I'm getting it," Brady yelled. He yanked open the storage closet door, dived in, and returned with Trevor's old blue backpack.

"What's the deal?" Trevor looked at Mom.

"I told him he could take it to school if he co-operated with getting dressed."

Trevor shook his head. That was Mom's method—bribing Brady into necessary evils. He didn't want the backpack anymore, but it irked him to turn it over to Brady.

Brady flaunted the backpack all the way to school. Trevor hoped Sister Suzanne could keep him from talking about it for the entire day. He was relieved when she took her students for a walk in the woods during last recess. Unless Brady managed to fall into the creek, maybe he wouldn't cause any more problems before they got home.

Trevor pushed Brady out of his mind long enough to enjoy fitting the binocular lenses into the holes he and Waylan had cut in a sheet of cardboard. They taped the cardboard over the office window accord-ing to Brother Willis's direction and fastened a sheet of white poster board on the wall across from it. When everything was ready, Brother Willis and the girls gathered in the office while the boys went outside and positioned themselves in line with the lenses.

It worked! They could hear the girls inside laughing about the upside-down boys reflected on the poster board. Then they traded places so the boys could see the girls.

At dismissal time, Sister Suzanne's students walked out first as usual. Trevor was following at the tail end of his own class when he happened to glance into the lower grade classroom. He stopped short.

Brady, alone in the room, was collecting a handful of items from the teacher's desk. Not noticing his big brother in the doorway, he dropped them into his backpack and proceeded to raid one of his classmate's desks.

Horrified, Trevor marched into the room. "Stop this minute!" He grabbed Brady's arm.

Brady yelped with surprise and anger. He dropped his backpack and swung his fist at Trevor who intercepted it with a firm grasp. Now Brady howled for real.

Brother Willis and Sister Suzanne appeared immediately. Trevor let go of Brady and stood aside. "I caught him stealing!"

"I'm sorry," Sister Suzanne said quietly. "I shouldn't have let him come back inside alone. He said he needed something."

Brother Willis pulled out two chairs from the class table. He sat down on one and pointed to the other. "Sit down, Brady." He kept his voice calm.

Brady obeyed.

While Trevor and Sister Suzanne stood watching, Brother Willis picked up the backpack and handed it to Brady. "Show me what you put in there."

Brady took out the items one by one and handed them to Brother Willis.

"Do they belong to you?" Brother Willis asked. Trevor marveled at how matter-of-fact he sounded, just as if he were asking if Brady had a cat at home.

Brady shook his head.

"Then you should put them back where you got them."

Brady got up and took several pens from the pile Brother Willis had made on the table. Carefully he placed them in Sister Suzanne's pen holder. He put her ruler and scissors back, then the stapler and paperweight. Finally he returned a box of crayons and an ice cream cone eraser to Cheyenne's desk.

Brother Willis motioned for him to sit down on the chair again. "You may not take things from other people's desks," he explained. "That is their property. If you need something, you must ask Sister Suzanne. Okay?"

"Uh-huh." Brady looked tearful. "But the other children have stuff to put in their backpacks. What can I take home?"

"You may take the papers I checked," Sister Suzanne said. "Remember the papers I gave you this afternoon?"

Brady shook his head. Sister Suzanne led him to his desk and showed him which papers she meant. Brady's face brightened as he jammed them into his backpack. "This, too?" he asked, pulling out a library book.

"Yes," she agreed. "Bring it back the next time you come to school."

Trevor guessed that she had given him these directions before, but they had gone in one ear and out the other. That's how Brady was at home. She would learn sooner or later that she had to see this child through every step.

"Ready to go now?" Brother Willis asked.

Brady nodded.

"There are lots of important things to learn at school, so keep coming back." Brother Willis ushered the two brothers out the door. "Have a good evening!"

Mom raised questioning eyebrows as they hopped into the van, but Trevor mouthed, "Tell you later." He had a satisfied feeling about the way Brother Willis had handled the matter, and he wanted some time to analyze how he had done it.

# NOTHING SO KINGLY

CHAPTER NINETEEN

## Homework Hassle

Without lifting her eyes to the orange maple leaves overhead or tuning her ears to the music of the creek, Jolene lugged her stack of books from the van into the classroom. She plopped them down on her chair and opened her desk to arrange them inside. After one glance around the room to make sure her classmates weren't looking, she flipped open her math book inside her desk and tried to rework the long division problem that refused to come out even after two decimal places. It would be so easy to just write a number and count it wrong, but her conscience wouldn't let her.

Jolene chewed the end of her mechanical pencil and tried again. The rest of her unfinished lessons haunted her. She wished Mother hadn't insisted on her help with that silly Tupperware party last evening. She had only made a fool of herself anyway when she dropped a stack of bowls on the floor. Cracking her knuckles, she attempted another problem. Still wrong! Pathetic! That was Mother's favorite description of goof-ups—Jolene's in particular.

Sensing a movement beside her, she looked up to see Brother Willis. Embarrassed, she dropped an arm over her work.

"May I help you, Jolene?" he asked.

Surprised at the kindness in his voice, she lifted the book out of her desk and laid it on top. Pointing at the division problems, she whispered, "They won't work out."

Brother Willis studied her work for a moment. "Oh, you're not far off. Here's a mistake in your sub-traction." He tapped the number with his pen.

Jolene corrected it and finished the problem easily.

"Got it!" he praised her. Then he showed her where she had erred on the other one. "Anything else?" he asked when she closed her math book.

Jolene hesitated. "Um, I don't understand my music."

As Brother Willis glanced at the clock, the bell rang. "I will be glad to help you right after devotions. Okay?"

Jolene nodded, but a hot feeling washed over her. Everybody else would hear! Oh, well, they already knew how dumb she was. What did it matter? But it would be hard to concentrate on what he was saying if she knew they were all listening.

Since it was Thursday morning, Sister Suzanne brought her students over for a song service with the upper grades. Jolene barely saw them. Several times she didn't hear the song number in time to find the right page before her classmates started singing. She had to remind herself to open her mouth and help. The thought of her inabilities loomed larger and larger. What if Brother Willis found out that she didn't have her English or science lessons finished either? She knew she should do them at recess, but Danielle or Everett would be sure to ask questions.

After prayer, Brother Willis dismissed the younger children and gave his own students their assignments for the day.

"Any questions before we start classes?" he asked. "If you don't understand something, please ask. It bothers me that some of you take so many lessons home that could be done here if you under-stood them."

Jolene wanted to look around the room, but she hardly dared. Who could he mean besides her? If he was saying this only for her benefit, she wanted to disappear.

"Jolene," he continued, "I'll answer your music question first. Then anyone else who has a question should be ready."

Jolene felt hot enough to faint as the teacher came to her desk, but she grabbed her music workbook and flipped to the right page. Across the aisle, Danielle's hand waved.

"Yes?" Brother Willis nodded at her.

"May I listen while you explain it? I'm not sure if I did it quite right."

"Certainly. I know this lesson is hard, and maybe I didn't explain it well enough. Is it number four, Jolene?"

"Yes," she whispered, not daring to glance around. But she could hear other desk lids opening and shutting. As Brother Willis re-explained the lesson, Danielle asked questions, too. Jolene relaxed as the terms became clear in her mind and she was able to complete the exercise.

Maybe she didn't need to be afraid of the new teacher after all. He didn't seem to think she was pathetic. He acted as if he expected everybody to have questions. And he was kind enough to answer them.

# NOTHING SO KINGLY

CHAPTER TWENTY

## A Horrible Story

Waylan scuffed his shoes back and forth across the front bar of his desk and tried to concentrate on the vocabulary for the new science unit: atoms, molecules, compounds, chemical formulas... But not a word registered.

All he could see was Mom collapsing on the kitchen floor, her face gray. He could hear Megan's scream and Othniel's sobs. He felt Cordell's arms clinging to his neck while Mom regained consciousness and Dad whisked her off to the hospital. Nobody cared about breakfast, but Gary said they should each try to eat one pancake since Mom had made them; they needed something for energy. Waylan had choked down a few bites and fed the rest of his to Cordell.

He flipped idly through his science book until

the diagram of a heart grabbed his attention. The top chambers were labeled *right atrium* and *left atrium*. The bottom chambers were called *ventricles*. Dad had used those words when he explained Mom's heart problem to their family.

The word *atrial* came from atrium. *Fibrillation* meant that rapid electrical impulses were causing the atria to contract too fast, which in turn made the ventricular rhythm irregular. If the atria did not pump all the blood into the ventricles with each beat, blood clots might form. Waylan hadn't understood why that was so serious until Dad explained that a blood clot could clog an artery and cause a stroke. Now Mom took aspirin to thin her blood. She also took another medication to slow her heart rate.

But Waylan knew what the doctor had told Dad: *If this medication doesn't work to correct her heart rhythm, we'll have to do an ablation.* How would their family survive if Mom had to spend a week or more in the hospital for surgery? Aunt Phyllis couldn't stay away from her bakery that long. Mom's sisters were all married and had children of their own. Dad's parents were too old to help, and Mom's lived too far away.

Waylan flipped a page in his science book. Oh, no. More demonstrations to prepare. He had thought this chemistry unit would be fun, but his concern for Mom was smashing everything else flat. Why couldn't Trevor just gather up the stuff on his own and show them all how it worked? He couldn't ask Dad to make a special trip to town when Mom was in the hospital.

In front of Waylan, Darica relaxed in her seat with one elbow propped on her desk. Tilting her tablet, she settled down to read what she had just written. Without thinking, Waylan let his eyes run across her page until two words jolted him like a pothole in the road.

**...mother's deathbed...**

He went back and reread the sentence: *With tear-filled eyes, Katie and her siblings gathered around their mother's deathbed, leaning close to hear her last tender words.*

Horrified, he dropped his head on his arm to avoid seeing any more. How could Darica write such terrible things? How could she even imagine them? He wanted to grab the tablet from her hands and rip out the pages. What if *her* mother was lying in the hospital right now? What if *her* mother had to choose between an operation and a stroke? Waylan shuddered.

When he looked up, Darica had started writing

again. Would she actually make the mother in her story die? If she did, she was heartless. Ten minutes later, when Brother Willis dismissed them for morning recess, Waylan still seethed at Darica.

He wanted to block his worries long enough to enjoy the dodge ball game, but everything went wrong. He and Trevor both landed in prison and yelled for the girls to free them. Jolene couldn't get her act together fast enough; Emelisa caught her before she managed to pick up a ball. Danielle grabbed a ball and threw with all her might, but Brother Willis caught it. The game ended.

The teams switched sides and began again. Waylan whooped when Trevor's first throw caught Brother Willis. When Emelisa threw a ball to free Brother Willis, Waylan intercepted it, sending Emelisa to prison as well. Danielle soon caught Everett. Now they were down to Darica.

"We've gotta get her!" Waylan yelled. Trevor joined him in hurling one ball after another at Darica, who gleefully pranced aside each time.

Her attitude infuriated Waylan. "Stop acting so smart!" he hollered. He slung a ball at her with all his might, not caring where it hit.

It smacked her in the face. When she yelped in pain, Waylan muttered, "You deserved it." He only regretted that she wasn't out, since face hits were against the rules of the game.

When the bell rang, Brother Willis fell into step with Waylan. At the entry door, he said quietly, "Stand aside, please."

The teacher waited until the other children were out of earshot. "It's not like you to get so upset. Is something wrong?"

"Everything!" Waylan burst out.  Then he clenched his jaw.  He wanted to pour out his troubles, but he knew his tears might come, too.

Brother Willis waited.

"Darica's nasty," Waylan managed.

"Because of the way she played dodge ball?"

"That and her horrible story."

"Her story?" Brother Willis sounded puzzled.

"That she writes when she's done her work."

Brother Willis was quiet so long that Waylan guessed he didn't know anything about Darica's story. Finally he asked, "What does her story have to do with you?"

Waylan knew he couldn't explain without losing control of his emotions.  "Ask her."

"Okay.  We'll talk more later." Brother Willis motioned Waylan inside.

# NOTHING SO KINGLY

CHAPTER TWENTY-ONE

## Darica's Day of Reckoning

At lunch time, Darica peered into the mirror as she washed her hands. Yes, she could see a bruise under her left eye where Waylan's ball had smacked her. Why had he acted so furious anyway? He usually liked wholehearted competition.

As she stepped out of the restroom into the hallway, Brother Willis motioned for her to come into the office. She went, wondering if he had an extra job for her, perhaps with the first graders.

Sure enough, he started by asking, "Are you caught up on all your lessons?"

"Ye—" she began, then faltered, remembering the guilt of an earlier day. "Well, I'm not quite finished my algebra."

"You often take it home, don't you?"

Darica's face felt hot. He had seen. "Sometimes

I do,"she admitted.

"Why, when you have plenty of study time here at school?"

Darica squirmed, wrestling with the truth. "Well, sometimes I don't understand it..."

"And you need help?"

"Daddy explains it to me." Then guessing at what the teacher might think, she added, "But he doesn't tell me the answers."

"I'm not opposed to that." Brother Willis seemed to measure his words. "But I would prefer if you asked for more explanation during class so that you could do your work here at school." He paused. "It seems that you spend a lot of time writing—stories, is it?"

Darica trembled. She had never been in such horrible trouble at school.

"Would you feel comfortable letting me read what you have written?" he asked.

Now she thought she would faint dead on the floor. She managed to stammer, "W-why? It's just a story I made up for my brothers and sisters."

"Well, it seems that something in your story has been hurtful to one of your classmates. I have no idea what without reading your story."

Darica felt sick on her stomach. "I'm--sorry," she choked. "I didn't mean to."

"I'd like to help you get things straightened out, but right now we should go eat. After lunch, I want you to put your story on my desk."

"Okay." Darica wondered how she would swallow one bite of lunch. She returned to the classroom, feeling like a creature from another world. Her classmates broke their chatter for a moment to glance at her, but no one asked any questions.

Darica opened her lunch box and stared at her sandwich. Who had she hurt? Who was upset at her? As she brushed a hand across her face, she accidently touched the bruise. Waylan! Had he been reading over her shoulder? She didn't dare turn around and look at him, but after a minute of concentration, she could tell that he was unusually quiet. What in her story could have angered him?

Suddenly she knew. The sick mom! Of course. Hadn't she based that part of her story on Megan's reaction to Mabel's heart problems? She hadn't heard any recent reports about Mabel's health, but maybe Waylan was still worried about his mom.

What should she do? What would Brother Willis think of her story? Would he consider it all a bunch of wild imagination and foolishness? She was trying to make it true to life, but maybe he would think she was overly sentimental in her descriptions of Katie's family. How could she make peace with Waylan? Tell him she would change her story, take out the sick mom part? What if he knew that in her imagination Katie's mom had already died? Would he think she was horribly hard-hearted? She had intended to prove the family's love by their pathos and tears.

There was nothing to do now except obey Brother Willis and hope for the best. After lunch she waited until last to leave her seat and quickly slipped her notebook onto his desk. Her heart pounded at the thought of exposing her imaginations to the teacher. Several times throughout the afternoon, she saw him pause at his desk to read. Oh, what was he thinking?

Finally, at last recess, Brother Willis told Trevor and Emelisa to go put up the volleyball net for their game. He sent Danielle and Jolene to clean chalkboard erasers and Everett to empty the trash cans. Then he came back and sat down in Trevor's desk across the aisle from his two remaining students.

"Now," he said, "I'm going to tell you what I think happened, and you may correct me if I'm wrong. Darica has been writing a fictitious story in her spare time, and she came up with the idea of incorporating a sick mother, possibly because of Waylan's mother's illness. Waylan happened to read that part of the story over Darica's shoulder, and it distressed him because his mother needed to go to the hospital this morning."

Startled, Darica shot Waylan a sympathetic glance. No wonder he was upset!

Waylan looked surprised, too, that Brother Willis knew.

"My wife called at lunch time to tell me about your mother," he explained to Waylan. "I'm sorry I didn't realize what your family went through this morning when she fainted. That was traumatic, wasn't it?"

Waylan whispered, "I'm afraid she'll need surgery if her medicine isn't working."

Everything was clear to Darica now. No wonder Waylan had felt overwhelmed. She pictured the scene in the Amstutz kitchen, and her heart went out to them. When Brother Willis asked if she had anything to say, she looked at Waylan. "I'm sorry about your mother. And about my story, too—that it made you feel bad. I didn't mean for that at all."

Waylan's troubled face relaxed. He ducked his head and murmured, "I forgive you. Sorry for that mean ball I threw."

Darica nodded. "It's okay."

"Thank you both for being willing to work through this," Brother Willis said. "Waylan, we'll do what we can to help your family. Don't worry about bringing things for the science demo tomorrow. I'll take care of that. You're excused for recess."

As Waylan left the room, Brother Willis handed Darica her tablet. "You may have this back. Keep on using your talent, but do your lessons thoroughly first. And here's the poem I want you girls to display on the next bulletin board." He handed her a paper. "The first verse can give you some direction in your writing. You may go to recess now."

Darica stared at the poem in astonishment. It was "Nobility"—Grandpap's favorite! The one she had already memorized. She had heard Trevor and Brother Willis discussing in literature class. She had never stopped to consider how it related to her writing. She slipped the paper inside her desk and put on her jacket while reciting in her head,

"True worth is in *being*, not *seeming*,
  In doing, each day that goes by,
  Some little good—not in dreaming
  Of great things to do by and by."

Yes, that made sense. It was the same thing Mom had tried to teach her—that it was more useful to serve the people around her than to dream up ways to become famous.

# NOTHING SO KINGLY

CHAPTER TWENTY-TWO

## Disturbance in Devotions

November rain beat against the window. Trevor sighed and dragged his hand across his eyes. What a way to start a gloomy day—hearing an exhortation about loving his brother!

Brother Willis sometimes explained the students' memory passage for devotions. This time it was Matthew 22:37-40, the two great commandments. To Trevor it felt like a personal attack when Brother Willis cited 1 John 4:20, "If a man say, I love God, and hateth his brother, he is a liar: for he that loveth not his brother whom he hath seen, how can he love God whom he hath not seen?"

Trevor rolled his eyes toward Brady who sat across the room. Did his teacher have a clue how hard it was to live with Brady, let alone love him? Worse yet, this impossibility plagued him every step of the way, every day of his life. Almost every Sunday, he heard something that reminded him of his need to surrender his life to Jesus. But how could he be a Christian if he had to live with Brady?

He tried not to remember how Brady had driven him to anger already this morning by dumping water on him at the breakfast table. Of course, Dad had blamed Trevor for starting the fuss, because he had refused to give Brady more Cheerios while he still had some in his bowl. Trevor clenched his fists at the memory, glad that he had managed to splat some of the water back at Brady before dashing upstairs for a dry shirt.

No, Brother Willis couldn't possibly understand, and he had no business sending Trevor on a guilt trip. Trevor closed his ears the best he could until it was time to stand for prayer. Afterward, Brother Willis called on Quentin whose turn it was to choose the closing song. When Quentin didn't respond, everyone turned to see what was wrong.

"I think I was going to say twenty-five, but—" Quentin's voice trailed off, and he motioned toward Brady who was clutching the songbook with both hands.

Trevor's blood pressure rose. He could tell by the look on Brady's face that he was not ready to give in.

"Brady, give the book to Quentin so he can choose

his song." Brother Willis kept his voice calm but firm.

Brady shook his head and gripped the book more tightly. Brother Willis walked over and held out his hand. Brady glared at him.

Trevor looked at Emelisa. Her face was red, her posture tense. Both of them could sense the storm brewing.

"Give me the songbook," Brother Willis instructed.

Rip! Out came a page.

Brother Willis waited no longer. He took Brady in one hand and the songbook in the other. "Come." He pulled Brady from his chair.

Brady tried to brace his feet, but Brother Willis maneuvered him through the doorway into the hall. After he closed the door, Sister Suzanne took over and led Quentin's song.

Trevor couldn't sing a note around the anger that burned in his throat. Right in front of everybody! Had the child no shame at all?

After the song, Sister Suzanne left the room for a few minutes. When she returned, she took her students with her to their own classroom.

The seven upper grade students looked around the room at each other. Trevor could tell that no one knew what to think or do. He was the oldest; would it be wrong for him to speak? He cleared his throat twice. When everyone looked at him, he said, "I'm sorry about that. Now let's get to work."

They all nodded, and Emelisa managed a faint smile at him as she opened her desk lid.

Ten minutes later, Brother Willis returned to the room and took up classes as if nothing unusual had happened. Trevor struggled to focus on anything besides the punishment he hoped Brady had gotten.

Rain still poured down at recess time, so Brother Willis decided they would play board games in the classroom. When he challenged Trevor to a game of fig mill, Trevor couldn't resist. As they wrapped up the first round, Brother Willis began a quiet conversation.

Trevor could hardly believe his ears when his teacher said, "I'm sorry I didn't act faster to keep Brady from getting so far out of hand in devotions. I know that was terribly embarrassing for you and Emelisa. Your parents told me about Brady's extreme reactions to some situations, and I know it's not because they haven't tried to teach him better. Actually, I worked with some children just like Brady in Ghana; their mothers drank alcohol and neglected them. I found them really distressing to deal with until I read and studied about their neurodevelopmental delays.

It took me a while, but I finally learned that some tactics worked better than others."

Trevor didn't know what to say, so he just nodded, remembering how Brother Willis's method had worked the day Brady was looting the classroom to fill his backpack.

"I thought of your challenge when I said what I did in devotions about loving your brother," the teacher continued. "I suppose that when Brady acts out like he did this morning, you find it difficult to love him."

"Of course," Trevor muttered. "He makes me angry."

"Well, what I want to say now is that you don't have to love the things your brother does. But if he can feel that you love him in spite of his problems, you have a good chance of helping him become a better person. At least you won't be making things worse." Brother Willis smiled at Trevor and motioned for him to start another game.

Trevor felt relieved when the bell rang. He needed time to think instead of trying to concentrate on a game. When the whole class was seated again, and Brother Willis called for sixth and seventh grade English class, Trevor propped his chin in his hands and tried to sort out what Brother Willis had said. Was it possible to help Brady become a better person? What about all the times he felt angry at

Brady? Was he sinning? Of course, he wouldn't dare ask anyone such a question. Not even Brother Willis.

· · · · ·

Sunday again. Trevor dreaded Sundays. For one thing, going to church triggered Brady's anxiety even worse than going to school did. Today, after the hassle of getting him out of bed and dressed in Sunday clothes, he had refused to eat breakfast until the rest of the family was ready to go. Then suddenly he wanted a bowl of Cheerios. Mom hurried back inside and returned with a small plastic container of cereal.

"Milk!" Brady kicked the van seat.

"No, not on the way to church." Dad buckled him into his booster. Mom handed him the container and went around the van to her own seat.

Dad had scarcely shifted the van into reverse before Cheerios flew everywhere. The girls screeched and started picking Cheerios off their Sunday sweaters. No one said another word on the ten-minute drive to church. Trevor seethed. Mom should never buy Brady another box of Cheerios.

At church, Trevor faced another quandary— trying to decide where he fit in with the other boys. Right now, he and Roger and Waylan sat together on the front bench. Roger grumbled about farm-ing; Trevor didn't have anything better to say about shed building. He heard Waylan's stories at school every day, so what was there to talk about on Sunday? Usually the three of them made a few boring comments to each other before Waylan drifted off to entertain the group of younger boys, and Roger went to join the older ones.

Besides Gary and Jayden, the youth boys con-sisted of Brother Mose's youngest son Mark, single at twenty-four, and sometimes Donovan's nephew Randall, who boarded with his grandparents to be nearer his work at James Ebersole's fabricating shop. These older boys all seemed to have oodles of friends in other congregations, fellows they had met at Bible school or hymn singings, who came for occasional visits. Trevor didn't blame Roger for trying to be in with them, but he didn't feel brave enough himself. Why would they want the tenth-grade brother of a brat to hang around and listen to their grown-up talk? Creekside needed a few more boys between thirteen and sixteen.

After Sunday school, Ernest Wadel stood up to preach. Trevor stewed about his distressing life until Ernest's words caught his attention:

"Here in Ephesians 4:26, it says, 'Be ye angry, and

sin not; let not the sun go down upon your wrath.'
Do you see the comma after the word angry?" He
paused to give his listeners time to look at their Bibles.

Trevor flipped to the verse and stared at it. How
did the preacher know his feelings?

Ernest continued, "I take this verse to mean that
there will be situations that displease us and make
us feel upset.  Anger is an emotion just the same
as happiness is. Anger itself is not necessarily a
sin. But we can't let anger control our actions and
cause us to sin. 'Let not the sun go down upon your
wrath' means we don't let anger lead to bitterness.
Instead we need God's help to master our emotions
and forgive the person who provoked us."

Trevor slouched on the bench. So, he was not
sinning just because he felt angry about Brady's bad
behavior. But on the other hand, he had not asked
God's help to forgive Brady. Did that mean bitterness was growing in his heart? Maybe God was
calling him to repent— No. He blocked the thought.
The whole thing was too big and hard and compli-
cated for a fifteen-year-old boy without any friends.

# NOTHING SO KINGLY

CHAPTER TWENTY-THREE

## The Teacher's Sister

As Jolene held the school door open for Jarrett, she peered over his shoulder to see if there were any boots on the carpet strips in the entry. Relieved to see that someone else's mother had deemed the first inch of snow worthy of boots, Jolene showed Jarret where to set his.

Sometimes Mother was so picky about clean, dry shoes that it was embarrassing. Just this morning, she had scolded Father for taking three steps across the laundry room after he walked in the snow. Jolene shivered at the memory. It had started with Mother telling Father to sweep the snow off the porch before he drove the children to school. Father had said it wasn't necessary, since they could get to the garage from the laundry room. Mother insisted that he do it, in case someone came to the door before he got back. So Father grabbed the broom and did it. Then he stomped his shoes on the concrete and stepped back through the laundry room to get to the garage. Unfortunately, Mother caught him in the act.

With her mind full of this scene, Jolene entered the classroom and nearly collided with an unfamiliar young lady.

"Good morning." The stranger stepped out of Jolene's way.

"G'morning." Jolene wondered why it was so important to say that at school. Nobody at home ever did.

"I'm Cassandra, your teacher's sister. Are you Jolene?"

Jolene nodded. Brother Willis had probably described his students to Cassandra and said, "Jolene is the fat, dumb girl in seventh grade." But maybe not. Cassandra was a bit plump herself, and Brother Willis was usually kind.

Jolene put her books away slowly, trying to think of something else to say. Finally she asked, "How long are you staying?" Then she felt like kicking herself; Mother would call that a rude question.

But Cassandra smiled. "I don't know. Maybe a long time if I can."

Jolene was puzzled. She had meant to ask how

long Cassandra planned to visit school, but Cassandra's answer implied more than that.

"Hi!" Darica burst into the room, followed by Danielle, who exclaimed, "It finally snowed!" Then they both saw the visitor and stopped short.

Jolene cracked her knuckles, wondering if she was supposed to make introductions. But before she could decide how to start, Darica said, "Oh, you must be Cassandra! I'm Darica, Donovan Wadel's oldest girl."

Danielle told Cassandra her name, too, and they kept up their cheerful chatter until Trevor and Emelisa arrived. Jolene could see that the Kurtz children were not at all surprised to find Cassandra in the room. Emelisa walked right over to her and began talking as if she had known her for a long time.

Baffled, Jolene went out to the hall for a drink. Had everybody been keeping Cassandra a secret from her on purpose, or had she not been paying attention well enough to catch on? And what was the real reason for Cassandra being here? To help slow people at school?

During devotions, Jolene watched Cassandra from the corner of her eye. Instead of being tall and dark-haired like Brother Willis, she was short and blond. Jolene didn't know anybody else in Brother

Willis's family, so it was hard to guess how old Cassandra might be. Where did she live?

Jolene hoped Cassandra would not stay in their room during math class and find out how poor she was at speed drills. What if Brother Willis decided to have Cassandra give her flash cards? Jolene remembered one of her lower grade teachers asking visitors to do that. To her relief, Cassandra followed Sister Suzanne's students to their classroom.

"Did you know Cassandra before?" Jolene asked Emelisa when she stopped to catch her breath on the snow maze at morning recess.

Emelisa nodded. "She went to Bible School with Stephanie, and she came to our house yesterday to meet Brady."

"Brady?" Jolene didn't understand.

"When he starts coming to school more days each week, Sister Suzanne wants a helper," Emelisa explained. "We figured it would work better to have somebody new instead of Stephanie or Veronica."

Now things began to make sense. Darica and Danielle knew about Cassandra because Donovan was on the school board. Jolene often wished Father would be on the board so she could find out what was going on, but she had heard him say that a businessman didn't have time for community service, especially if it didn't pay.

Cassandra spent a short time visiting Brother Willis's classroom while the younger children finished their lunch. When Emelisa mentioned their plans to change the bulletin board display during afternoon recess, Cassandra asked eagerly, "May I help you?"

"Sure!" Darica spoke for all of them.

Jolene found herself nodding, although she doubted whether Cassandra noticed her.

When recess time came, the girls spread their prepared decorations on the class table. Following Brother Willis's instructions, they had enlarged the "Nobility" poem for display. Darica had planned a snow theme for which she and Danielle had cut all sizes and shapes of snowflakes. Emelisa had fashioned a cotton ball snowman and a balsa wood sled.

Cassandra pointed to the title's snow-topped letters. "That's a perfect heading!"

"Jolene did that," Danielle said. "Her brother showed her how to make a banner on his computer."

Cassandra acknowledged Jolene's accomplishment with a cheerful nod. "You might become a graphic designer if you keep practicing."

"No fair. My dad won't let me use his computer yet," Darica complained.

"Life is fair; it just isn't equal," Cassandra said.

"I read that in a book, and it helps me not feel jealous of others."

Cassandra jealous? Of what? Jolene wished she could ask. But Cassandra was still talking as she picked up the sheets of paper and read them. "I remember this poem! 'There's nothing so kingly as kindness.' That's my favorite line."

• • • • •

On the way home from school, Jolene said, "Brother Willis's sister Cassandra came to visit school today. She helped us with the—"

"She visited our room more than yours," Jarrett butted in.

"Cassandra Yoder?" Mother sounded unimpressed. "She's not Brother Willis's sister."

"But—she said she was," Jolene stammered. "She didn't tell me her last name."

"She moved in with Willis's parents at Edgemont because she couldn't deal with her own family's problems," Mother said. "Now as soon as Willis brings his family to Creekside, she shows up here."

Jolene felt a need to defend her new friend. "The school board asked her to come help Sister Suzanne with Brady."

Mother muttered something like, "What an idea!"

But Jolene's mind was already jogging down another trail. Cassandra's family had problems. What kind of problems? Did she know how it felt to be the oddball at family gathering? Did her mother tell her how dumb she was? Did her parents scold and fuss at each other?

Maybe, for the first time, Jolene had met someone who could understand. Would she dare tell Cassandra about her struggles?

# NOTHING SO KINGLY

## CHAPTER TWENTY-FOUR

## A Maid for Mom

"Sister Cassandra, Sister Cassandra, Sister Cassandra comes today..." Megan hopped around the kitchen on one foot, stomping out the accents to her self-made song.

"Do you like having two teachers in your room?" Waylan asked as he stepped out of his boots in the laundry room and carried two jugs of milk to the kitchen sink.

"Sure! We don't have to raise our hands so long."

Waylan laughed. "When I was in first grade and my teacher didn't answer my hand, I huffed and puffed like the big, bad wolf. She said I would just have to wait longer if I did that." He looked around. "Where's Mom?"

"In there." Megan pointed toward the living room.

"Then you should stop thumping around."

Waylan frowned as he put his barn clothes in the closet and washed his hands. He dreaded finding Mom on the couch first thing in the morning. That confirmed the need for the heart ablation the doctor had scheduled yesterday. He had hoped that they could all work hard enough to keep Mom's heart from getting worse.

Hearing Cordell's voice, Waylan hurried to the living room. Sure enough, Mom was lying on the couch with her youngest son crawling all over her, begging for attention.

"Cordell!" Waylan scolded. "Don't hurt Mom." He scooped up the toddler and set him on his shoulders while analyzing Mom's condition. Her face looked pale. "Did you faint?" he asked her.

"Not quite. I thought I might, so I stopped here."

"Everett should have taken Cordell away. Who's going to take care of him all day?"

"Dad will help, but I really do need to find a maid before I have to go to the hospital again." Mom sounded exhausted.

"Everett should be ready for school by now, so I'll take this bunny rabbit along up to our room." Waylan trotted up the steps with Cordell sitting on his shoulders.

Below him, he heard Mom asking Megan,

"How many days each week does Sister Cassandra come to school?"

"Three," Megan said. "Monday, Wednesday, Friday."

Reaching the bedroom door, Waylan almost collided with Everett who burst out, "When is Mom's operation?"

Waylan pushed past him to see a calendar. "It must be February 6. Next Thursday—isn't that what Dad said?"

Everett shrugged. "I wish it wasn't so soon."

"I guess we should have worked harder to take care of her," Waylan said. "Right now somebody needs to entertain this baby while I shower." He dumped Cordell into Everett's arms and hurried to collect his school clothes.

At supper the next evening, Mom told the children that Sister Cassandra had agreed to come work for them on Tuesdays, Thursdays, and Saturday mornings for as long as Mom needed her help.

"Will she come tomorrow?" Megan asked.

"No," Quentin said. "Tomorrow is Wednesday, so she goes to school."

Mom nodded. "That's right. She'll start here on Thursday."

Waylan looked around the table at his siblings. Of course, Quentin and Megan were delighted with the idea; they considered Cassandra their friend. He saw Gary and Roger raise their eyebrows at each other and tried to imagine how they would relate to a girl several years older than themselves. Everett looked utterly distressed. Waylan felt that way himself: they hadn't done a good enough job of helping Mom, so she had to hire a maid. When Dad excused them, he hurried to clear the table. He would show Mom that he could do dishes as well as Cassandra or any other girl.

Mom smiled at him as she snapped lids on bowls of leftovers. "You boys do so well at helping me, but you'll be okay with a girl doing some of this housework, won't you?"

Waylan shrugged. It would be selfish to say that Mom shouldn't get a maid. "We're used to her at school now, so it won't be too weird. But, Mom—" he hesitated, "what is the deal with her? I mean, some people are saying she is Brother Willis's sister, but somebody else said she's not. Is she adopted, or what?"

"I guess you could call her his foster sister. She lived with Willis's parents for quite a few years now. I think she moved in a little while before Willis and Cheryl got married." Mom wiped the blue-flowered plastic table cloth.

"What's wrong with her own family?" Waylan clattered tumblers into the dishwater.

"It's a sad story," Mom answered. "Her dad was unfaithful to her mom, and neither of them treated their children the way Christian parents should. Cassandra's sister married a divorced man. People who cared about Cassandra took her to live with the Brubakers. From what I've heard, they did her a lot of good just by treating her kindly."

"Oh." Waylan didn't know what else to say. Doing without Mom when she was in the hospital was bad enough; he didn't want to imagine moving to another household. He must do everything he could to keep things running smoothly for his family, even if it meant working with a maid.

When he and Mom were finished in the kitchen, he ran upstairs to find Everett. To his surprise, his usually carefree brother huddled at the plastic folding table in the corner of their bedroom, crying.

"Everett! What's the matter?"

"Everything!" Everett jabbed his pencil toward his math book. "I'm tired, and I didn't get my lessons done today, because these old decimal problems wouldn't come out even. And isn't that horrible about Cassandra coming to work for Mom?"

Waylan sighed and sat down on the chair at the other end of the table. "I guess we have to accept that Mom needs somebody more than just us."

"She probably won't let me do anything in the kitchen, and she'll feel dumb with a bunch of boys around, and we'll have to stay a mile away from her, and that'll make us feel dumb in our own house, and we'll never have any fun anymore." Everett finally ran out of breath.

Waylan didn't know what to say. Everett was probably right. He didn't know if Cassandra had any experience with brothers or not. All he knew was what Mom had just told him about Cassandra's family. And that was what he had come to tell Everett.

"She's used to living with people who aren't her family. Brother Willis isn't her real brother."

Everett sat up and wiped his eyes on his shirt sleeve. "Huh? Wha'd'ya mean?"

Waylan repeated what Mom had told him.

"That would be nasty," Everett said. "Glad our dad and mom aren't like that."

Waylan nodded. "Here, I'll help you figure out your math."

# NOTHING SO KINGLY

CHAPTER TWENTY-FIVE

## Food Fixing Fantasies

"Hey, girls, tell me what you think of this idea!" Cassandra popped into the upper grade classroom on Friday morning before the bell rang. "I'm going to be helping Larry's family for a while. You know Mabel's having a heart ablation done next week, right? I thought it would be fun to get together at Brother Willis's place tonight and make a bunch of food for Larry's. I'm not so great at putting whole meals together while I'm trying to manage laundry and cleaning and all that, so I'd like to be prepared ahead of time."

Darica pictured buckets of cookies, foil pans of casserole, a bowl of potato salad. "Sure, that would be a fun party! Shall we bring stuff along? We have extra potatoes."

"Veronica's at Bible school, but Stephanie would

probably like to help us," Emelisa offered. "We can bring apples. Mom just said yesterday that they're getting soft and need to be worked up."

"Let's bake cookies," Danielle joined in. "Boys always eat lots of cookies."

"Great ideas!" Cassandra was obviously pleased with their enthusiasm. "You can all bring whatever your moms are okay with."

Darica looked around for Jolene. "Do you want to help?"

Jolene shrugged. "If you want me to."

Darica raised an eyebrow at Danielle. Just last night they had tried to decide what was wrong with Jolene. She used to talk a lot about what her mother thought was the right way to do things, but lately they didn't hear much out of her. It was hard to know if she was upset at them or if she just didn't care.

Cassandra said quickly, "Of course, we want you to come, Jolene. And bring whatever you come up with. I must get back to my classroom, but I'll see you around 6:30 if it's okay with your moms."

Darica couldn't think of any reason Mom wouldn't let her and Danielle go. They didn't have anything planned other than the regular chores, and it wouldn't take more than five minutes for Dad or Mom to drive them to Brother Willis's house.  She found it hard to concentrate on devotions.  As soon as Brother Willis was finished, she pulled out a scrap paper and began a list:

> *cheddar chowder*
> *potato salad*
> *molasses cookies dipped in white chocolate*
> *fudge puddle bars*
> *sandwich rolls*
> *apple dumplings*

She imagined how impressed Larry's boys would be when Cassandra arrived with all this.  Of course, she would tell them who had helped her.  Waylan and Everett might bring some of the food to school in their lunches, and Everett would be sure to announce how much he liked it.

When Brother Willis called for algebra class, Darica knew she'd better stop dreaming and buckle down to lessons.  But lunch time brought the food subject to mind again when she saw Jolene open her lunch box.  "Meager fare" was the best way to describe Jolene's lunch.  A plastic bottle of Gatorade, one slice of white store-bought bread with a piece of watery lunch meat, and a packaged granola bar.

Darica barely kept the words, "Where's your

fruit?" from slipping out of her mouth. She set her own golden apple in Jolene's view. Why in the world wouldn't somebody as rich as Jolene's family buy apples? Or grapes? Or oranges?

Danielle beat Darica to the front seat of the van after school. "Mom, Cassandra came up with a great plan! She wants us girls to help her make food for Mabel."

"She's going to be their maid on the days when she's not teaching," Darica said. "Can you take us over to Brother Willis's after chores tonight?"

Mom nodded as she shifted into drive. "Cheryl called me about Cassandra's idea. She though the moms should know what was going on and make some plans ahead of time. I offered potatoes, so we're responsible for the potato salad ingredients."

"Can't we do more than that?" Darica felt irked that the ladies had taken over. "Danielle said she wants to bake cookies. I made a list of some of our favorite recipes that I'm sure Larry's family will like, too."

"We planned one thing for each family involved," Mom said. "I'll show you the list when we get home."

Disgruntled, Darica plopped back in her seat. If Mom already had an agenda, there wasn't much hope of convincing her to change her mind to something more spectacular.

The plan Mom showed them was simple:

*D&D—potato salad*
*S&E—apple Danish*
*Jolene—chickenetti*
*Cassandra—cookies*
*Cheryl—breakfast food*

"But, Mom, that's not enough to last a big family very long," Darica protested. "See, here's what I was thinking." She laid her own list on the table.

Mom read it and shook her head. "I don't think your evening will be long enough for all that. Potato salad has so many steps; I was thinking it would be wise to cook our potatoes ahead of time. Besides, we don't need to give them a whole week's supply at once. They have other friends and relatives who will want to give food, too. Now, you'd better get your barn chores done."

"I wish we girls could make our own plans," Darica grumbled to Danielle as they dipped cows.

Danielle shrugged. "At least Mom didn't say we can't go. I think Jolene's afraid her mom will say no. Did you see how hesitant she acted?"

"Yeah. Her mother probably still can't stand the idea of going inside that Ridge Road house."

Danielle laughed. "I forgot about that. Something Jolene told me the other day made me think her mother doesn't like Cassandra."

Darica rolled her eyes. "What next? I wish Judy wouldn't be so critical of everybody else."

Neither of them knew what Judy was planning for the evening.

# NOTHING SO KINGLY

CHAPTER TWENTY-SIX

## Nothing So Kingly As Kindness

"If you bring the apples, I'll carry this," Emelisa called to Stephanie. As she slipped into her coat, a blast of wind whipped in the back door with Trevor.

"Horrible weather," he grumbled. "Dad said I had to stock the pellet stove in the shop so it's fit to work out there tomorrow morning. Where are you going?"

"To Brother Willis's to help Cassandra make food for Larry's." Emelisa picked up her box of ingredients.

Trevor grimaced. "Everybody makes such a huge deal over them. Just because they have a sick mom. We have a sick brother; does anybody do anything about that?"

Emelisa stared at him. "Why, yes. Brother Willis and Sister Suzanne do the best they can. That's why they got Cassandra in."

"Cassandra, Cassandra," Trevor growled.

"Everybody acts like she is the greatest thing since the ballpoint pen. I heard she has problems herself."

"Let's go." Stephanie slung her purse strap over her shoulder as she grabbed the dishpan of apples. Emelisa followed her to the car.

"What's wrong with Trevor anyhow?" Stephanie started the car.

Emelisa tried to decide how to explain what she knew about Trevor's moods. "Well, for one thing, he feels like Dad doesn't care how embarrassing Brady is."

"At school?"

"Mostly, I guess."

"Did he do something bad today?" Stephanie wondered.

"Could've been worse, I guess. He caused a commotion in the hall at the drinking fountain. Brother Willis had to go separate him from the other little boys."

"It doesn't bother you as much as it does Trevor?"

"I don't know." Emelisa couldn't explain it. Sure, she wished Brady wouldn't misbehave, but it didn't make her angry like it did Trevor. He seemed to feel—what was it? —threatened, maybe, by Brady.

To Stephanie, she said, "Cassandra is nice about working with Brady. That helps."

"Why is James's van parked here?" Stephanie wondered as they turned in at Brother Willis's place. "Is Judy staying?"

Emelisa said nothing.  She remembered the look on Jolene's face when Cassandra had invited them.

Donovan's van pulled up, and Darica and Danielle jumped out.  "What's the deal?" Darica motioned toward James's van.

Inside, their question was answered.  Before Emelisa had time to take in her surroundings, Judy turned from Cheryl's mixer and announced, "I decided we could make sandwich rolls, too, if I stayed to help.  I can easily get my thirty-minute recipe stirred up and baked till you get your potatoes cooked and all that."

Emelisa did not miss the look that passed between Darica and Danielle.  Jolene sat on the far side of the table, carefully breaking a few sticks of spaghetti at a time into a kettle.  She did not look happy. Cassandra stopped scooping cookie dough to welcome her friends.  She fetched Stephanie a kettle for cooking Danish and offered Darica a spot at the sink to peel potatoes.

"Mom already cooked them." Darica set an eight-quart bowl on the table and unsnapped the lid. "It's faster that way.  I'll pop the skins off now and finish cooling them in the fridge."

Judy frowned as she peered into the bowl. "You cooked them with the skins on? They won't come out clean and white like peeled ones."

Darica tossed her head. "Mom says this is quicker and healthier. Anyway, you don't see what color they are in potato salad, because the eggs make the dressing yellow." She took the empty ice cream bucket Cheryl handed her and deftly began slipping skins off the partly-cooled potatoes.

"Eggs in the dressing?" Judy looked even more scandalized. "How is that safe to eat?"

"They're not raw!" Danielle took up for her affronted sister. "We always make cooked dressing; it's nice and creamy."

Judy went back to measuring flour.

Emelisa started peeling apples while Danielle put the eggs on the stove to hard boil.

"Do you want to make the dressing, or shall I?" Darica asked.

"You may," Danielle said. "I'll help Emelisa."

"You're welcome to use this." Cheryl fastened her hand-crank peeler to the corner of the table.

"It's just like ours." Danielle slid an apple onto the prongs. "This will make our job go fast."

Judy came to the table to dump her roll dough

into a stainless-steel bowl. "That's the cheap kind," she said. "I just bought one that attaches to my KitchenAid mixer."

When Danielle rolled her eyes, Emelisa's stomach quivered. She saw Jolene cringe. Cassandra said, "Judy, if you're finished with the mixer bowl, I'll wash it for Cheryl, so she can start her coffee cakes. Jolene, you can cook your spaghetti on this burner as soon as the eggs are done."

Emelisa watched Cheryl and Cassandra with admiration. Even with Judy running the show in their kitchen and making negative comments, they seemed relaxed. Cheryl occasionally checked on her family in the living room.

"Here, Jolene, you don't need to stand and watch the spaghetti," Judy directed her daughter. "Open these cans of mushroom soup and chicken and dump them into this bowl. Make sure you don't cut your finger on a sharp edge. We don't want to waste money on stitches."

Emelisa didn't miss the blush that spread across Jolene's face. Judy tossed aside Cheryl's hand-held can opener and pulled an electric one out of the large box she had brought along. The atmosphere felt brittle with tension.

Cassandra came over beside Jolene. "That looks

like a handy gadget.  May I see how it works?"

Jolene showed her.

Emelisa took a deep breath and said, "We're ready to shred the apples now."

"Are you used to a KitchenAid shredder attachment?" Cheryl asked, apparently remembering Judy's peeler. "I'm sorry, but that's something I don't have yet."

"You don't?" Judy exclaimed.  "How do you ever live without one?"

Cheryl laughed. "I couldn't even take my KitchenAid with me to Ghana, and I survived.  Willis wants to buy me a shredder sometime."

"Why not chop the apples with a knife?" Stephanie suggested. "We like them that way in Danish just as well as shredded."

"I'll help you," Danielle offered.  "Then you can help me chop celery."

Jolene ventured closer to her classmates, and Emelisa gave her a knife to join the apple slicing. Judy was busy shaping rolls, but within minutes, she came over to Jolene. "Not so fast," she hissed. "Keep them small and even."

Emelisa wanted to say, "Hers are as good as mine," but the words stuck in her throat.  Her heart burned with sympathy for Jolene.  How could she hold up her head with such a belittling mother?

Darica was shelling hardboiled eggs. Judy checked on her next. "Make sure you wash them thoroughly. That time we ate egg salad at your place, I bit on a piece of shell, and later I lost a filling from my tooth!"

Darica's mouth opened and closed. Her face turned redder than Emelisa had ever seen it—whether from anger or embarrassment she did not know.

"How are you going to finish the potato salad without a shredder?" Judy asked next.

Darica looked to Cassandra for an answer. Cassandra looked at Cheryl.

"I'd use my grater." Cheryl pulled it out of a drawer. "But it's up to you. Maybe you'd rather take your potatoes home and shred them."

Darica shrugged. Emelisa knew she was afraid to express her opinion with Judy at hand.

"Do you want me to help you?" Cassandra asked.

Darica nodded and got the potatoes from the refrigerator. Emelisa held her breath until the two were working smoothly together. Judy didn't try to interfere with them. Instead she checked up on the celery chopping—to make sure they had perfect eighth-inch pieces, Emelisa guessed.

She felt like sagging in relief when they had washed the last cooking utensils and arranged all the food in bowls, bags, or ice cream buckets.

"It'll be fun to surprise Larry's family tomorrow morning." Cassandra's eyes sparkled. "I'll let the children help me carry all this food in from my car. And I'll tell them how each of you helped. Thanks so much for your contributions!"

"Yes, thank you all for coming," Cheryl said as they put on their coats.

Darica stood close to Stephanie. "Mom said to ask if you can drop us off on your way home. If that doesn't work, we can call her."

"Sure!" Stephanie opened the door and stepped outside. "Come jump in my nice cold car!"

The girls followed her quickly.

"Anywhere to get away from Judy!" Darica slammed the car door.

Emelisa gave a long, shivery shudder. "How can Jolene stand it?"

"I'd run away if I were her," Danielle declared.

"Where to?" Darica asked. "Her mother would be on her tail in a minute!"

"She could come to our house, and we'd defend her."

"Seriously, girls," Stephanie spoke up, "the kind of friends you are to Jolene can really make a difference in her life. She needs to know that you love and accept her in spite of her mom's problems."

"Like Cassandra does," Emelisa said.

"Yes! She worked hard to keep the evening pleasant in spite of Judy's nasty remarks," Stephanie agreed. "She knows how Jolene feels."

"Because she had a bad homelife, too?" Darica asked.

"Yes, she told me a little about her childhood. She said it was tough getting moved out of her home, but that was her first chance to learn about kindness and forgiveness."

"But Mom says a bad childhood is what made Judy unkind." Darica sounded puzzled. "How could the same thing make Cassandra nice?"

"She gives the Brubakers the credit for that. They took her in when she was sixteen and showed her kindness like she had never imagined."

"'There's nothing so kingly as kindness...'" Emelisa murmured.

"Is that a poem?" Stephanie asked, slowing down at Donovan's driveway.

"Yes, we're memorizing it at school."

"Well, Judy probably never got enough kindness," Stephanie said. "And now it's hard for people to show it to her, because of her porcupine quills. But it's not too late for kindness to make a difference in Jolene's life."

"Yeah, we'll try," Darica said, as she jumped out of the car. "Thanks, Stephanie."

"See you, Emelisa," Danielle added.

# NOTHING SO KINGLY

CHAPTER TWENTY-SEVEN

## A Drink in the Desert

Jolene cried herself to sleep. Mother had spoiled the whole evening. Her friends would never like her again. She had seen Darica and Danielle roll their eyes; she knew what they thought of Mother and her opinions. Emelisa always tried to be kind; Jolene guessed that was because she knew how it felt to be embarrassed by a family member. And what must Cassandra be thinking? Jolene had so badly wanted her for a new friend.

Mother woke her at six. "I forgot to tell you that Father wants me to go with him to the trade show he has scheduled for today. It's three hours away and starts at ten, so we need to leave shortly. Jayden's going to work in the shop; we're taking you and Jarrett to Grandpa Saunder's. Hurry up and get dressed."

Jolene groaned. Why would anybody hurry to go

to Grandpa's? Did Mother really want her to spend the day doing what Aunt Rochelle did? Stuff that made her feel guilty? Jarrett would be happy; he liked the television, electronic toys, and video games at Grandpa's. He wasn't old enough to understand what the church leaders said about such things.

When Father and Mother dropped them off at Grandpa's half an hour later, Aunt Rochelle met them at the door. "Did you have breakfast?" she asked.

"No." Jarrett wrinkled his nose. "Mother said you would give us some."

"Well, it's too early to wake the Old Ones, or they'll be grumpy. Get in my car, and we'll go get something. Waffle House or IHOP?"

"What's IHOP?" Jarrett wondered, running over to his aunt's red Mustang.

"International House of Pancakes." Aunt Rochelle motioned for Jolene to jump in the front passenger seat. Taking the driver's seat, she turned the key. Engine and music started simultaneously.

Jarrett bounced on the back seat. "This is fun! I want a sausage burrito, Shelly. Which place can we get 'em?"

Aunt Rochelle laughed. "Mickey D's. You don't want anything better than that?"

Jolene hunched in her seat. This was not fun; it

would look weird—two Mennonite children with a woman in jeans, T-shirt, and earrings. What if they met somebody they knew?

Aunt Rochelle turned the music up louder as they sped into town. First, she swung in at McDonald's drive-through where she ordered Jarrett's burrito and a cup of coffee for herself. "Do you want anything here?" she asked Jolene.

Jolene cracked her knuckles and shook her head.

Walmart was next up. "Come along," Rochelle said. "I'll grab a couple things in in here; then we'll go get more food."

Aunt Rochelle led them to the cosmetic aisle. Jolene waited nervously while her aunt selected lipstick and eyeshadow. She felt even more uncomfortable in the entertainment section where Jarrett scanned the television screens that lined the back wall.

By the time they entered IHOP, Jolene's stomach churned at the smell of food. To be polite, she ordered two pancakes with gravy and nibbled them down while Rochelle and Jarrett tried out several options.

When they finally returned to the car, Jolene noted the time with dismay. Only 8:52. What a long day this would be!

"Are we going back to Grandpa's now?" Jarrett asked.

"Let me check Ken's message. He might want to meet me somewhere." Aunt Rochelle scrolled through her texts. "Okay, he says after lunch at the library. A bunch of our buddies will be there."

Jolene wondered if Ken was the same boyfriend her aunt had brought to family gathering—the one with ear pins. She cracked one knuckle after another until she realized that Aunt Rochelle was looking at her. "What?"

"I asked if you want to go along."

Jolene shook her head. "I don't like to read."

"You don't have to. I thought you'd like to meet my friends."

Jolene shook her head harder. "They won't want me."

Grandma grumped at them when they got home. "Such a long time to be out goofing around, Shelly. Next thing you'll be begging for money again. Did you kids get anything decent for breakfast?"

"Yeah," Jarrett began eagerly, "we went to the pancake hopper—"

Aunt Rochelle burst out laughing, and Grandma said shortly, "You still have jelly on your face. Go wash."

Jarrett headed for the kitchen sink, but Grandma caught him by the arm. "Bathroom is the place to wash."

Jarrett darted back the hall, and Jolene heard the water running. When he returned, he announced, "I'm going down with Gramps." He thumped down the carpeted steps to the basement living room where Jolene knew Grandpa would be lounging in his huge recliner in front of his television.

Jolene sighed and turned to Grandma. "Do you have work for me?" It was what Mother had taught her to ask. She already knew what the jobs would be: empty the dishwasher, reload it, vacuum the floors, clean the three bathrooms... Apparently Aunt Rochelle didn't like these jobs. Meanwhile Grandma would attend to all sorts of details such as picking dead blooms from her violets, dusting her knickknacks, and polishing her mirrors. But at least Jolene had something to do.

At lunchtime, she plopped onto a bar stool and accepted a slice of pizza hot from the oven. As she nibbled, she admired the tidy rooms opening off the kitchen. Grandma was as fussy about her house as Mother was, and Jolene felt good about serving her well enough to avoid complaints.

When Grandma came back up from carrying pizza to Grandpa and Jarrett, she announced, "Now that the cleaning's done, I want to go to the grocery store and the beauty salon. Can you come along and help me with my groceries?"

Jolene's pizza suddenly clogged her throat. The beauty salon! Was Grandma serious? That would be as bad as going to the library with Aunt Rochelle.

"I guess," she murmured. Why did Mother put her in these hard places?

On the way to town, Grandma listed excuses for going to the beauty salon.

"I don't like when my hair looks yellow, so I get them to whiten it. They have some good anti-wrinkle cream, too. And it's so nice to have someone trim and polish my nails."

Jolene didn't mind the grocery shopping. Grandma pointed out the items she wanted— mostly the same brands Mother chose—and Jolene arranged them in the cart. When they reached the check-out, she stared in amazement. Cassandra! She was moving through the line right beside theirs. Would she notice them?

A minute later, she did. "Hi, Jolene! Helping your grandma today?"

Jolene nodded.

"She sure is," Grandma said. "Pretty much has all my work licked. Guess I'll give her the rest of the day off when we get home."

"My parents aren't getting back until tonight," Jolene explained.

"Hey, maybe you want to help me?" Cassandra sounded eager. "I worked for Mabel this morning, so I need to do my school work this afternoon."

An escape route! Jolene looked at Grandma. "Could I?"

"I don't care, if you help me get these bags into my van first. And make sure you call your mom in a couple hours, so she knows where you are."

Safe in Cassandra's car ten minutes later, Jolene let out a sigh of relief.

Cassandra grinned at her. "What's that mean?"

"You saved me from going to the beauty salon. I knew I would feel so dumb waiting for Grandma there. I mean, why does she have to go to places like that?" She glanced at Cassandra to see if she looked shocked.

Cassandra started her car. "I know exactly how you feel. When I was a girl, my parents went places and did things I knew they shouldn't. Sometimes they made me go along. If I said anything, I got my mouth slapped for talking back."

"Jarrett and I had to go with Aunt Rochelle this morning," Jolene said. "It would've been fun if she was a Christian, but I felt odd walking through Walmart with her."

Cassandra braked at a red light. "Did you know my sister Charlene isn't a Christian either? I wish we could do things together, because she's my only sister, but like you said, it feels odd to run around town with her. And most of the other things I do, she doesn't care much about."

"What about your mom?"

"Not good." Cassandra drove away from town. "She won't let Dad live with her; says he never was anything but trouble. We're all kind of scared of her. I actually haven't talked with her for several months, because all we end up doing is arguing. Jolene, I felt bad for you last evening—the way your mom talked."

Jolene felt tears welling up. "It's because I'm such a dumb girl."

"No! Don't think that!" Cassandra exploded. "That's how I used to think, and it almost drove me crazy. It's not true. None of us want to admit that our parents have problems, but it doesn't do any good to blame it on ourselves either. Was that your mom's mom you were with today?"

Jolene nodded.

"Can you imagine how your mother felt when she was growing up? I can. Everything was confusing.

She couldn't depend on her parents for help to do right. Now she's trying to do right herself, but she struggles in her mind. Don't you think?"

Jolene nodded. Cassandra's ideas made sense though she would never have been able to put them into words. She rode in silence a while, soaking them up. As they turned in the school driveway, she asked, "What if people think I act like my mom?"

"'True worth is in being, not seeming,'" Cassandra quoted. "That's what my second mom— Rosanne Brubaker—taught me. You know, the poem on your bulletin board?"

Jolene nodded. She had memorized it, but she didn't really understand it.

"We need to practice being kind and honest," Cassandra explained. "People can tell if we're sincere." She parked the car and gave Jolene a smile. "I liked you right away when I met you, even though I could tell there was something you were scared of." She opened her car door.

Jolene blinked. She wanted to say something, but her mouth felt too dry. She got out and followed Cassandra to the porch. As soon as Cassandra had unlocked the door, Jolene went to the fountain for a long, cool draught of water. As she turned away from it, she noticed the name on the front: *Oasis.*

She remembered that word from social studies class. *A drink in the desert*, she thought. *Just like Cassandra.*

# NOTHING SO KINGLY

CHAPTER TWENTY-EIGHT

## To Work and Wait

Waylan propped his chin on his hand and tried to focus on his English assignment. Why must he diagram independent and subordinate clauses today of all days? His mind kept straying to Mom in the hospital. Was her surgery over yet? He had asked Dad if he could call at lunch time, but Dad said she might not be out of recovery yet.

"Try not to worry," Dad had encouraged him. "I'll talk to you as soon as school is over." The whole family had prayed together, a special prayer that God would bring Mom safely through surgery and heal her according to His will.

Waylan let his eyes roam the room. He saw Trevor raking his fingers through his hair and frowning in distress. Trevor would be a better friend if he weren't so pessimistic. In Waylan's mind, Trevor fit in the same slot as Roger—always grumpy. Was Everett heading in the same direction? This morning he had cried again in the bedroom. But that wasn't being grumpy, Waylan decided. That was being anxious, and he really couldn't blame Everett for that. Not when he felt so tense himself.

Waylan idly skimmed the poem on the bulletin board, his thoughts lingering on the last verse:

> "Through envy, through malice, through hating,
>     Against the world, early and late,
>   No jot of our courage abating—
>     Our part is to work and to wait."

He remembered how Brother Willis had explained those lines: Ugliness, mistreatment, and failure caused by sin in the world are not good reasons to give up. A noble person has courage because of his faith in God. He will keep working and waiting during times of difficulty.

That meant times like right now, didn't it? Could he keep working and waiting with courage while his mother was in the hospital? He knew that was what Mom would want him to do. She had given them each a smile and encouraging words this morning when they parted. Waylan wondered how she could be so brave.

"No jot of our courage abating—Our part is to work and to wait." That's what Mom was doing. He could do it, too. Might as well get this homework out of the way so he could help with chores and babysitting this evening.

When dismissal time finally arrived, Waylan rushed to the van. Dad was driving!

"Mom is doing great!" He answered Waylan's unspoken question immediately. "The doctors are satisfied with how everything went."

"Her heart is fixed? Forever and aye?" Waylan asked eagerly.

Everett jumped into the second seat and leaned forward to hear Dad's answer.

"We hope so. Heart arrhythmias can reoccur as a person grows older, but the doctor feels that it's corrected for the time being."

"How long will she have to stay in the hospital?" Everett wondered, moving over so Quentin and Megan could get in.

"If everything goes okay tonight, she can come home tomorrow."

"Who's with her now?" Waylan asked.

"Barbara Lehman. She said she could stay all

night, so I could be home with you children."

Waylan nodded. Barbara was a widow who had been Mom's friend for years. She lived almost as far away as Aunt Phyllis, but her schedule wasn't as demanding.

"Are Othniel and Cordell still at Carlin's house?" Quentin wondered.

"Yes," Dad replied. "Shana said she'd be glad to babysit them as much as we need her to," Dad explained. "But she'll bring them home tonight so they can sleep in their own beds. Cheryl came over with Cassandra to do the laundry and put our supper in the oven. They brought more food, too—mostly stuff for your lunches."

"Yippee!" Everett rattled his empty lunch box. "Just so it doesn't have girls' cooties on it."

"Why do you say that?" Dad wondered.

"Darica and Danielle bragged about how they all got together with Cassandra and made food for us. I told them it tasted like their fingers."

"Everett! That sounds ungrateful." Dad gave him a reproachful look in the rearview mirror.

Everett wilted a little. "I think they knew I was just joking. But they acted like boys can't make food, and that embarrassed me."

Waylan understood. "You do a great job with

food," he assured Everett. "They just want to make it easier for you. I thought when you said 'Yippee!' that you meant you were glad for something to put in our lunches. Aren't you?"

Everett shrugged, opened his library book, and began to read.

Two hours later, Waylan strode through the darkness back to the milking parlor. One bottle calf yet to feed. He hoped Dad and Roger had milked the fresh cow by now. He had asked for the milk earlier only to have Roger snap, "Why can't you ever be patient?" That was Roger nowadays—always irritated.

Swinging open the door between the milk house and milking parlor, Waylan stopped short. All the cows were through and the milkers hanging, but Dad and Roger stood close together, talking. It almost looked like Roger had been crying. Neither of them paid any attention to Waylan, so he picked up the pail of milk and walked away.

In the milk house, he poured milk into a bottle, popped the nipple on, and stood thinking for several minutes. He had assumed that Roger was worried about Mom, but maybe he had something bigger on his mind. Why was Roger so grumpy? Was it because he had never given his heart to God? Whatever

Roger's problem was, talking with Dad was the best thing for him to do. Waylan went to feed the calf.

When he returned the empty bottle to the milk house, Roger was there, removing the pipeline from the tank and starting the wash-up system.

"I'm sorry for grouching at you," he said, looking embarrassed.

"That's okay." Waylan waited a moment to see if he would say more. But Roger was still Roger, the brother who found it hard to express himself.

Waylan wasn't at all surprised when he ran downstairs to fill Cordell's sippy cup at bedtime and overheard Dad telling Mom on the phone, "Something good did come of all this; Roger became a Christian tonight."

# NOTHING SO KINGLY

## CHAPTER 29

## Essay Assignment

B rother Willis called the class to order after morning recess. "Today instead of your usual reading and literature classes, we're going to do something special together," he announced. "We've been busy working through our regular curriculum and not taking much time for the arts. That word might make you think of drawing and decorating." He gestured toward the bulletin board, and the girls grinned at each other.

"However," he continued, "music, poetry, and composition are also included in the arts. Before the girls take down this display, I'd like to do one more thing with the poem we discussed and memorized." He stepped closer to the bulletin board and waited for their full attention.

"I want each of you to give some thought to what

is most meaningful to you about this poem. You may choose a line that stands out to you and explain what you like about it. Or think of an experience in your life that is related to something expressed in this poem. When you put these thoughts into words, you will be writing what we call a personal essay."

He paused to look at the older students. "Some of you have studied essays in literature class, and you already have a feel for the content of a personal essay. So that you all understand what kind of writing I want you to do, I'm going to read to you what I wrote about this poem."

Darica sat up straight and looked around at her classmates. They all looked as eager as she felt to hear what kind of writing Brother Willis did. The teacher took a quick drink from his thermos and began to read.

### Fair Measure

"Nobility" has long been one of my mother's favorite poems. During my childhood, she recited pieces of it according to the circumstances. The two lines at the beginning of the second verse were probably the ones I heard most often. "We get back our mete as we measure—We cannot do wrong and feel right."

She was trying to teach me an important truth,

but I didn't catch on until one day in my early teens after I made a serious mistake.

The relatives on my mother's side had all come to Pennsylvania for a cousin's wedding. This was rare, since there were thirteen children in her family, and they lived with their families in six different states. I was excited about entertaining my cousin Cyrus from Wisconsin. I knew that Brian, my Pennsylvanian cousin, wanted to spend time with Cyrus, too, but Brian and I didn't always get along so well. I suppose that was because I was the only boy in my family during those years, and Brian tried to act like a big brother by bossing me around.

When Mom said that Cyrus's family planned to stay with us, I decided that would be my chance to tell Cyrus what kind of person Brian was. The very first evening Cyrus spent with me, I showed off my new bike, my dog, and my ball glove. "This stuff always makes Brian so jealous," I said. "I sure hope we don't have to spend much time with him while you're here. He always thinks he can decide what we're going to do, just because he's three months older than I am. I call him Brian the Big Boss."

Cyrus didn't say much, but I didn't notice because I was so busy trying to impress him.

The very next evening, we all got together

at Grandpa's, and Brian took over as usual. "I put the volley ball net up as soon as we got here, so let's go play before it gets dark," he said. "Angela and I are going to pick teams."

I was so angry. Why couldn't I be a team captain instead of my big sister? I knew what Brian had up his sleeve. Sure enough, he chose first and got Cyrus on his team. Then he refused to pick me, so I had to play on Angela's team. Worse yet, I overheard him telling Cyrus, "Willis thinks he's a great player, but he's just a big bragger. Selfish, too. I get so tired of him."

I played as hard as I could to show Cyrus that Brian was wrong. But my angry shots sent the ball out of bounds, and our team lost. I stomped away and found a corner where I sat down and cried. Right then, I was convinced that Brian was in the wrong; he had spoiled everything.

It wasn't until weeks later, when my mom quoted her poem for some other reason, that the words, "We get back our mete as we measure" suddenly brought those ugly scenes to my mind. First, I had tried to turn Cyrus against Brian. In return, Brian had tried to ruin my friendship with Cyrus. Indeed, I had gotten back my mete as I had measured.

Darica let out her breath slowly and looked around at her classmates. Most of them were staring at Brother Willis as if they had never seen him before. And it was true—he had shown them a younger version of himself that they had never imagined.

Brother Willis smiled at their surprised faces and called on Everett who had raised his hand.

"I can hardly believe you ever acted like that!" Everett exclaimed.

Darica grinned. Trust Everett to express the sentiment of the whole class!

"That's why I wrote it," Brother Willis said. "And that's why it's called a personal essay. The reader will learn something about the writer that he can connect with. He will see what made the writer change and grow. Do you think you can put something like that on paper? I'm sure you've all learned some lessons in life, haven't you?"

Darica nodded. She knew already which lines she was going to use: "...Not in dreaming of great things to do by and by." She looked at Emelisa across the aisle and guessed that hers would be "There's nothing so kingly as kindness." What would the others write about?

She raised her hand. "Will we get to read each other's essays?"

Trevor scowled and shook his head. Waylan nodded, his eyes sparkling with interest. Everett contorted his face. Emelisa raised her eyebrows and grinned. Danielle gave Darica a look that said, "You know yours will be the best." Jolene sat staring at the bulletin board as if she expected it to spell out her essay for her. Darica wondered if any of the poem was simple enough for her to understand.

# NOTHING SO KINGLY

## CHAPTER THIRTY

## Personal Essays

### Bargains for Blisses

*By Trevor Kurtz*

I'm no good at driving bargains and I wouldn't recognize blisses if I saw them on the shelf at Walmart, so the poem is correct in saying we can't make bargains for blisses. I never went fishing with a rod let alone a net, so that part applies, too. And yes, I miss out on the good stuff. It makes no sense to say "the thing our life misses helps more than the thing that it gets," except that I would probably be better off with no brother than one that causes me so many problems. It doesn't matter what I do for him, he socks me in the stomach, so the "doing as we would be done by" doesn't apply here. Not much chance of nobility in the life of Trevor Kurtz.

## Great Things

*By Darica Wadel*

I love books. Ever since I learned to read, I have wanted to write books. Reading a biography of Harriet Beecher Stowe really made me feel as if writing a book could change the world. If I wrote a good enough book, I might become famous.

When I started making up stories, they were not realistic. My characters did great things such as rescuing their friends from danger at the risk of their own lives. Sometimes they escaped from enemies through secret tunnels. Other times a missing person such as an Indian captive turned up miraculously still alive and was reunited with his family.

This school term I am learning that it is more important to be a responsible person every day than to dream "of great things to do by and by." This phrase comes from the poem "Nobility" which our teacher asked us to memorize. If I am making up stories when my mom wants me to cook supper or do the laundry, I am dreaming instead of doing good in the present.

It has also been a temptation for me to write stories at school instead of doing harder lessons such as algebra and music. But I am responsible to do my best in subjects I don't like as well as the ones that might lead to "great things to do by and by."

Most important of all, I want to make sure I am being kind when I write. If my writing hurts other people, it is certainly not a "great thing" to be doing.

## Nothing So Kingly as Kindness

*By Emelisa Kurtz*

My favorite line in "Nobility" is this one: "There's nothing so kingly as kindness." I really admire people who can be kind to everyone, because some people are not easy to be kind to.

For instance, some younger children get upset and do ugly things to others. If a little boy scratches and kicks you, it is hard to feel like being kind to him. You know that it is wrong to fight back, because the Bible says, "Love your enemies." But to actually be able to do a kind deed for him is like something a king would do for a poor beggar in his kingdom.

Sometimes older people are unkind, too. They must not realize how their words hurt the people around them, so they keep criticizing people that they think aren't good enough. It is really hard to forgive these unkind people, because it seems like they should know better. But it is still kingly to be kind to them, because God wants us to forgive them.

## Courage

*By Waylan Amstutz*

We had to have courage when our mom was in the hospital. We were worried about whether her surgery would go okay and if she would get better. Thankfully she is not having heart problems anymore now, although she does take medicine for her heart each day.

We had a lot of work to do by ourselves while she was in the hospital, and it was kind of hard to keep our minds on our work. That was when I thought about the last verse of the poem on the bulletin board. It says, "No jot of our courage abating—Our part is to work and to wait."

## What I Can Do

*By Danielle Wadel*

The part I like best in "Nobility" is where it says, "The air for the wing of the sparrow, The bush for the robin and wren." Brother Willis explained that not everybody has the same place in life or the same talents. Sometimes I wish I could do everything as well as my sister, but I'm more sitting in the bushes while she is flying. I didn't like that until one day she couldn't figure out how to fix the doorknob that came off. She asked me, and I showed her how. She thanked me and said that was something I could do better than her, and that is why she needs me to be her sister. That made me feel good.

## Being Kind

*By Jolene Ebersole*

The poem talks about being a kind and honest person. That is how Cassandra is. She likes this poem and she talks about it. One time she was talking to me about how people know if we are trying to do right, and she said that is what the poem means about being, not seeming. I don't really understand it all but I just want to be a kind person that is doing right.

## My Mom and Dad

*By Everett Amstutz*

"And nothing so loyal as love." That is the line in the poem that I like best. It makes me think about my mom who is the best person in the world. She always loves us even when we are naughty and that helps us be good. When she was sick, she still worked hard because she loves us. We try to show her that we love her too.

"And nothing so royal as truth" makes me think about my dad. He told us a story about one time when he was little and told a lie. Grandpa punished him and he said that was so my dad wouldn't grow up to be a bad person that got put in jail. My dad learned a good lesson from that and he taught us to tell the truth, too.

**About the author:**

Darletta Martin started writing books as a teenager. Memories of her own school days along with sixteen years of teaching experience make it easy for her to write about life in the classroom. She lives with her husband and two sons on a farm near Smithsburg, Maryland. They sell reading material through Book Depot and serve food at Trackside Kitchen.